Solidarity and Survival
A Vision for Europe

JOHN LAMBERT

Avebury

Aldershot · Brookfield USA · Hong Kong · Singapore · Sydney

Published by
Avebury
Ashgate Publishing Limited
Gower House
Croft Road
Aldershot
Hants GU11 3HR
England

Ashgate Publishing Company
Old Post Road
Brookfield
Vermont 05036
USA

British Library Cataloguing in Publication Data

Lambert, John
  Solidarity and Survival: A Vision for Europe
  I. Title
  321.04094

ISBN 1 85628 871 4

Library of Congress Cataloging-in-Publication Data

Lambert, John
  Solidarity and survival: a vision for Europe / John Lambert.
  p. cm.
  Includes bibliographical references.
  ISBN 1-85628-871-4 : $55.95 (approx.)
  1. European federation. 2. European communities.
  3. Antinuclear movement--Europe.
  I. Title
  JN15.L32 1994   94-9862
  327.1'7'094--dc20   CIP

Printed and Bound in Great Britain by
Athenaeum Press Ltd, Newcastle upon Tyne.

Contents

Preface

This book is a bi-product of several decades of involvement with the attempt to unite Europe, both within the institutions of the European Community and with movements (against nuclear power and nuclear weapons) which had to operate in the European dimension.

As a journalist working for ("Agence EUROPE"), a specialised news service, I followed the negotiations for British membership of the Common Market, that were cut short by de Gaulle's veto. As a press officer for the European Commission, I had a ringside seat for the clashes between de Gaulle and the "Europeans". Then came a decade as European correspondent of the Sunday Times, followed by a sabbatical year writing a book about what was happening to farming under the Common Agricultural Policy. With the arrival of the first directly elected European Parliament, I was able to help several small parties (Italian left, regionalists, Danish anti-Marketeers, and later the "Greens") get together to defend their interests.

In several of the events mentioned in the book, I was an active participant - marching against the French fast-breeder reactor site at Creys-Malville, and the German site at Kalkar; helping to launch and run the European Conventions on Nuclear Disarmament, held for ten successive years in different European cities; helping to build a sheepfold on the Larzac plateau, in central France, that was a symbol of the shepherds' resistance against expulsion by the French army.

My thanks are due to all those who over the years, wittingly or not, have helped me enrich my understanding of Europe. I must mention in particular Hendrik Brugmans, former Rector of the College of Europe; Emanuele

Gazzo, editor of EUROPE; and Bino Olivi, spokesman of the Commission during the dramatic events of the 1960's. Heinz Kuby and Erich Kitzmüller helped me to view society with a more critical eye.

But above all, this book would not have been possible without the activities of the **agenor** group (named after the mythical Greek whose daughter Europa was carried off by Zeus), the commitment of its hard core members and the loyalty of its wide circle of supporters. I am glad to have been one of the founders of that group, which for 25 years has been a catalyst for cross-frontier contacts and activities. Our publications - first a review, later one-off pamphlets, and now well past the hundred issues - have kept up a flow of critical thinking about the integration process. We like to feel that we have been able at times to act as a leaven in the increasingly remote and bureaucratic institutions of the Community. Recent moves towards a European super-state have made the voice of an opposition (however faint) all the more necessary. It is in that spirit, and drawing on the thinking and experience of the **agenor** group, that this book has been written.

Lastly, thanks to all those who helped with producing the book, not least at the daunting inter-face between typescript and production. For all errors and inaccuracies, the author bears sole responsibility.

Introduction

Humanity today has the skills and the resources required to provide the basic necessities of life - food, clothing, warmth and housing, health care, education and information - for everyone on earth. It has, too, an accumulated experience of ordering human affairs, of techniques of communication and methods of government, that could enable the world to live in peace, without inequality or injustice, war or violence, and at harmony with the bio-sphere of which we are part. The planet can offer infinite beauty and unending sources of wonder and of pleasure. Nor are there limits to the magic of man-made culture, which progress with communications puts within the reach of all.

So Utopia is within our reach. Yet at the same time the whole world is caught up in a multiple crisis of self-destruction. Human society is undergoing poverty, sickness and starvation; economic exploitation and the resulting inequality and conflict are creating stresses that are all too quickly becoming untenable. At the same time the bio-sphere - the planet with all its inter-acting life forms and infinite complexity - is the victim of irreversible damage - self-inflicted, committed by mankind, and threatening to lead to catastrophes that can spell the end of life on earth. Ways of jiggering with natural processes of reproduction and evolution have become the peak of "progress", with attempts to impose ethical controls lagging behind events, and feeble when compared with the commercial interests involved. The initial historic wave of nuclear disarmament leaves the risk of nuclear conflict intact. A never-ending supply of sophisticated weaponry encourages armed conflicts where negotiation and compromise could bring an end to violence. The search for effective peace-keeping machinery is at its beginnings, the United Nations open to domination by the USA and its "allies".

The list of dramatic crises, each of which alone would be a daunting

1

challenge, is enough to cause despair or nurture a sort of fatalistic cynicism. The failure to master these crises contributes in turn to another, fatal trend - the declining credibility not just of politics but of democracy as a system.

At the origins of the process of self-destruction is the prevailing economic system, built around the accumulation of wealth and of power. This system increasingly escapes the checks and balances that have partially tamed it, at the national level, in times past. To master such concentrated economic power as has been accumulated by banks and multinational companies, operating world-wide, political control must be exerted at the level where that power is exercised. But precisely at that level, beyond the nation state, the institutions and the instruments are lacking. With no framework in which to act, thought-out alternative policies are lacking too.

This book brings together, intentionally, three orders of problem that are seldom related to each other:
- the vast economic and social problems - foremost among them unemployment - that are common to countries throughout the world;
- the ecological threats that hang over the planet;
- and that great political failure of the second half of the 20th century, the attempt to unite Europe.

What is most important is precisely the juxtaposition of these problems. It reflects the conviction that the survival of human society on a peaceful basis not only depends on devising workable institutions, but is inextricably linked with a new approach to economic issues (above all the place of work in society) and a harmonious relationship to the planet as a whole.

Like people in all parts of the world, the Europeans have to adapt to an ever-smaller world. High-speed transport, but above all breakthroughs in communications technology, have abolished distance, and released economic forces operating world-wide from any effective political control. Symbolic of this are the giant oil-tankers, re-routed on the high seas on the basis of computerised calculations of profit margins on the forward markets; symbolic, too, is the fact that those same tankers, escaping strict regulations because they are registered under flags of convenience, are the cause of accidents that wreak ecological havoc. Financial speculators, hounding a limping national currency in the hopes of making profits from its devaluation, operate round the clock as one stock exchange takes over from another. The challenge is to instal - or restore - democratic control over these forces.

For those who live in a federal state, and are used to decisions being taken at different levels, the addition of a "European" dimension for policy-making

- and in the long run planetary dimension too - raises no difficulty of understanding or involvement. But for those who came of age politically in a centralised nation state, the transition can be difficult. This is especially the case for France and the United Kingdom, with their long traditions of playing an important international role, and resources and influence enough to nourish the illusion of being "medium-sized powers". Their reticence about "loss of sovereignty" (when what is at stake is a pooling of sovereignty to achieve things which countries cannot do successfully on their own) has been a hindrance to the unification process, and remains so today.

The incapacity to practice effective, peaceful self-government, at the appropriate level, is perhaps the over-riding problem for much of the world. Most developing countries are caught in the debt trap, devoting to paying off their loans the resources that should be devoted to meeting the needs of their own people. The "developed" countries of western Europe are no longer in a position to vaunt their traditional systems of more or less managed economies with matching parliamentary democracy. Political systems which until recently seemed deep-rooted and if anything only too stable, have been undermined by corruption, buffeted by sudden massive swings of opinion, and are under threat from growing social problems to which they are failing to provide answers: unemployment, migrations, the rise of racism... In central and eastern Europe the great thaw that followed the end of east-west ideological confrontation has shown that freedom from repressive centralist régimes is not in itself the guarantee of a workable democratic alternative. The realisation is dawning that the material benefits associated with the consumer society cannot be imported simply by abolishing the role of centralised government and opening up a "free market" economy.

What undermines democratic systems throughout the world is the incapacity to "deliver the goods" - a manifest incapacity to solve either economic problems - above all unemployment - or those frightening world-wide environmental problems - "green house effect" and shrinking ozone layer - of which public opinion has begun to be aware. Shifts in the dimension in which economic power is wielded, from the national to the international and/or world level, have enabled those who wield that power to "escape" the democratic political control that in the past could be exercised, partially at least, at the national level.

At the world level, no action is foreseeable: national governments may be prepared to act through the United Nations for humanitarian or peace-keeping operations, but it is a different matter when it comes to controlling economic forces. There is no matching willingness to envisage acting through the

United Nations to exercise control over those economic forces, operating at the world level, that are responsible for many of the world's most pressing problems of destruction and injustice. This is a reflection of the immense power that lies concentrated, and can be mobilised to head off any threats. The forces engendered by the prevailing economic system are aware of the threat to their domination from any effective political organisation, either at the world level (in the long run) or the level of an economically powerful regional unit, such as the European Union (on a shorter time scale), that had a mandate to monitor their activities.

There are two basic questions that emerge. The first concerns institutions: how to enable political force to be exerted (for democratic control), at the level at which economic power is being wielded. The second question concerns the content of policy: if the necessary institutions could be developed (and in time !), what guarantee is there that they would answer the challenges - challenges against which democratic systems at the national level have so far proved inert and ineffective. In European politics, as in the emerging world-level politics, there is a need for political vision, combining new institutions with far-reaching new policies.

There is a seismic divide emerging along the double fault-line of attitudes to other people and attitudes to the eco-sphere. On one side are those who accept the prevailing credo of unlimited material consumption, and whose attitudes to the rest of the planet (people and ecological surroundings) are imperialistic: on the other side are those who see solidarity among people and wise husbandry of the planet as fundamental values. Only if this divide comes to be understood, and can be convincingly presented in terms of political choices, is there a chance for survival.

The idea of this book sprang from a concern shared by many, about the striking incapacity of the Europeans to exert on the world scene the influence that their material weight and their collective experience would justify; and a lack of the imagination and the involvement need to solve the internal economic and social problems of their rapidly changing society. This situation constitutes a challenge to work out new, federal institutions and at the same time new policies responding to the crucial problems facing Europe and the world.

But such issues can only be meaningfully discussed within a clearly identified political context. It seemed necessary to provide a backdrop, suggesting how and why the attempts of the Europeans to unite have failed; and what chances there are, if any, of their facing up to their responsibilities in the future.

The result of this complex background is that the book shifts from one level to another. It can be read as a modest "traveller's guide" to the old Community and the new "Union", the shortcomings of the first and the potential of the second. Or it can be taken as an effort (necessarily pretentious) to help the Europeans grope towards a vision - one that can inspire them to take up those responsibilities.

It is a book written for the ordinary citizen, as a contribution to understanding of the European political scene. It is not aimed primarily at the "Eurocrats", big and small - though there lies behind it a cautious hope that it can stir some of them to think in broader and more visionary terms about the utopia that is possible, and the contribution that they can make to creating it.

1 Crises and challenges

The world today faces series of crises. Some of them stem from the fact that in a society built around the work ethic, technical developments are making work increasingly superfluous:and the resulting unemployment generates a host of related problems. Other crises have their origin in the growing incapacity of government to ensure peace and prosperity in the place of conflict, injustice and suffering. Others again concern damage being done to the eco-sphere, - damage which when taken all together amounts to a threat to the very survival of the planet, human life included. There are many others: the elimination of thousands of rare and wondrous species, from insects existing in a few square metres of rain forest, to birds that migrate the length of the planet; the potential for conflict over resources, above all of water; the potential for misuse of the technical breakthroughs in genetic engineering.... If there is one term that adequately describes what is afoot, it is "self-destruction".

For what is happening is not being visited upon us by irate gods. We cannot attribute it to the intervention of evil forces from space. Nor is it the result of happenings on planet earth or in the universe that are beyond our control: passing comets or secular climatic changes. On the contrary, it is the activities of people - the institutions in which they are organised, the techniques that mankind has invented, and the values and priorities which guide their action - that are responsible. If solutions are to be found, awareness of the threats that hang over us is only the beginning. What is needed is a broad acceptance of our global responsibility - for both economic activity and our relationship to the environment and a sense of urgency. That in turn means changes in prevailing attitudes and in policies that have hitherto gone unchallenged. But such changes are possible only if there are democratic institutions capable of offering people a choice between

7

alternatives, and carrying out the changes once decided.

The many crises that face us - social, economic, ecological or political - are not new. The concerned citizen and newspaper reader will know of the existence of most of them, at least in broad terms. Each is a special source of concern to one or other group of people - from trade unionists worried about unemployment to bird-watchers keeping vigil over the nest of a threatened species. But rarely is there any consensus about its relative gravity or urgency. Equally rare is any effort to present them all as facets of a single crisis, and think in terms of an overall strategy to face up to that crisis. This may result from a natural human tendency to shun problems which seem to be beyond our grasp, and turn aside from situations which would leave us no peace of mind. It may also stem from a taboo that rules out frontal attacks on multi-national banks and companies, or the prevailing system which leaves them free to pursue their own goals with little or no concern for the fate of workers or the unemployed or for what is being done to the environment. Whatever the explanation, the lack of an overview stands in the way of the sense of overall urgency, deriving from a common impending fate, that will be needed if policies and attitudes are to be radically changed.

Lester Brown, the founder of Worldwatch and one of the first to present an overall picture of the ecological crisis, called his first book on the threats that hang over the eco-sphere "The Twenty-Ninth Day". If water-lilies are spreading across a pond, doubling each day the surface they cover, and we know that the whole pond will be covered on the thirtieth day, when will it be half full ? Answer: on the 29th day. The message is clear: the realisation of the urgency of the situation is likely to come too late. Lester Brown's concern is primarily with ecological disaster and destruction: the process is all the more frightening when other destructive trends are taken into account: the decline in humankind's capacity to govern itself, the spread of local and regional conflicts, and the consequent crumbling of the credibility of democratic systems.

Merely to call the roll of crises is to feel a wave of despair. Each individual who becomes aware of the crises faces a fundamental option: to seek a personal way of escape as part of a privileged minority within the prevailing system - the "Maldive Ostrich" option"; or to accept an involvement in facing up to at least some aspect of the over-riding challenge.

For those in the economically developed countries, the problem with both the most immediate and the most profound impact, on individuals and communities, is *unemployment*. Yet it is only the most striking example of a deeper problem: the lack of political control over economic forces. The economic system now prevailing world-wide is based on work as a central value. But work is being systematically eliminated under the constant pressure of competition, concentration of capital and control, and technical breakthroughs. Increased productivity (meaning more produced with less work) is presented as a criterion of successful management, at the same time as each successive loss of jobs is regretted (but referred to as though it were the result of some neutral, uncontrollable force): the paradox is so gross that it goes unnoticed.

Unemployment stands out amongst the many parallel crises of industrial society as perhaps the cruellest in its impact. Our attitudes to work may be ambiguous, and for a growing proportion of those who do work, the whole process - early to rise, travel under stress, work under pressure, question marks over the future - may be one they would glad be rid of, for it is neither enjoyable nor rewarding. A job that is rewarding is a luxury and an exception - often to be paid for at a high price in over-work and stress. So in a society officially sacrificing to a work ethic, where to work is the stripe on the sleeve of normality, life without the need to work is a kind of unavowed utopian dream.

But at the same time it is precisely in the work-oriented society that not having a job has a deep negative significance. For those who feel themselves physically and mentally healthy, unemployment is a token of uselessness. Governments, parties and trades unions, in the age when "manpower"(sic) was short, cultivated the idea that there is a right to work. Such a commitment is not compatible with an economic system based on competition, low costs and maximum productivity - in other words, elimination of jobs. The needs of the economy may have changed, governments, parties and unions may have reconciled themselves to high levels of unemployment: for those seeking in vain (or having just lost) the job they feel to have a right to, the frustration runs deep.The negative effects spread out like ripples from each person on the dole. Not having a job - not being found useful - undermines self-respect: it is a source of humiliation in the eyes of families, partners, children, neighbours - and former colleagues. But it also means poverty and material hardship, harder to bear in a society that attaches status to conspicuous consumption. Unemployment is saving up for Christmas presents, not having a video-recorder, going without meat several times a week, or giving small children Coke because it is cheaper than milk.

But there is also social impoverishment. Unemployment is sitting for hours in the pub or the café, doing nothing, whilst your friends are away at work.

9

At one end of the scale of victims are older workers, sacked precisely at the time when their capacity to adapt is declining, and the chances of getting another job are minimal. At the other end are those leaving school with the knowledge that even with basic qualifications their chances of getting a job are slight, since firms prefer to take on those who have already acquired experience. Unemployment, or the threat of it, spreads its tentacles to the "privileged third" who are at the prime of life with their feet firmly on the career ladder. Ever sharper competition on costs, against a background of unemployment, means that any job at any level is at risk. "Re-structuring" in an effort to stay in the competitive rat race may mean a strategic decision to replace workers by robots, to shut-down a plant that is the mainstay or a local economy and a source of jobs for hundreds of families, or off-loading managerial staff as a result of mergers. The stress of living this sort of threat can have a ruinous effect on health or family life. When a cyclical upturn in an economy does occur, firms tend increasingly to opt for "flexibility". That means avoiding binding contracts or long-term commitments towards workers whom they take on. This leaves them free, if there comes a down-turn, to off-load those who helped them make the most of the temporary improvement.

It is one aspect of the indictment of our society, where solidarity is no longer a recognised value, that so little is done to prepare people for using more "leisure time". Neither the state nor employers have seen this as part of their responsibility. Yet the problem was foreseeable, with the onset of far-reaching mechanisation, long before the advent of an irreducible block of unemployment - just as a new challenge can be foreseen as computerisation renders the majority of clerical jobs superfluous.

There is a vast potential for job creation not in treating the aged and the unemployed as a new class of consumers, but in developing facilities and skills for which there is a real need: education and training at all levels; environmentally friendly tourism, which includes everything from permanent residence in a warm climate to planet-wide travel; broader development of humane surroundings for the old and for the handicapped...

Instead, it is the private sector that has moved in to exploit the unemployed, as one of the many groups - along with teenagers, the elderly and the old - to be targeted to achieve a maximum of individual consumption. Government, at the local or the national level, has missed the chance of developing new forms of solidarity, with the unemployed involved in helping other groups in society, and being in their turn accepted and treated as citizens with equal rights.

A related aspect of the same crisis is the relentless elimination of a secular social and cultural heritage, and of collectivities with their hard-won stores of wisdom about relations within and between human communities. Faced with the destructive impact of "progress," peoples that have so far remained isolated from, or have resisted, the pressures of the western consumption-dominated model are increasingly struggling for their cultural survival. In most cases they seek to make their own thoughtful choices about what aspects of the western consumer-oriented life-style they will adopt, adapt or tolerate, and what they will reject.

In the industrialised world too the cultural identity of whole regions is being wiped out under the pressure of economic developments. The steady elimination of rural society in large parts of Europe is but one example. Skills once passed on from craftsman to apprentice are now disappearing, or are preserved only by the patronage of the richest élites. With them go parts of our heritage, and work that was enjoyable and rewarding. It is not a question of artificially preserving the traditions of the wheelwright when wheels can be mass-produced in metal and rubber, but of retaining the work of carpenters, joiners, and cabinet-makers, that can enrich ordinary people's lives with objects of use and beauty.

In the richer and the poorer parts of the world alike, collectivities are falling apart, as human relations are dictated increasingly by the pressure of consumption, vehiculed by television, life-styles are steam-rollered by the car and its attendant culture, the super-market and its inevitable uniformity. Villages that were at the centre of farming and fishing communities are increasingly deserted - only to be re-colonised, if the area is attractive enough, by the city élites taking over farm houses or cottages as holiday residences or places to which to retire, but not being absorbed into the local culture.

Destructive production

The second major crisis is that of the environmental destruction caused by every stage of economic activity: acquisition of raw materials, production processes, distribution (packaging and transport), and the waste generated by each operation. Under the prevailing economic system, maximising consumption (which in turn implies maximum production) is a legitimate goal because it raises the "standard of living".But it also yields maximum profits which lead in turn to maximum accumulation of wealth and of

11

economic power and influence."Growth" remains the formal political goal of the free market system, and production is the yard-stick of growth. Other criteria such as well-being, levels of health and education, state of the environment... are not taken into account. But growth results in inequalities - and in destruction.

The environmental crisis can be addressed from several different angles. One is the impact of a particular industry or sector of activity. Oil and the oil industry provide one of the most striking examples. Their impact on the environment covers CO_2 emissions from vehicles, the volume of plastic waste, and pollution of the seas - from vessels illegally washing out their oil tanks on the high seas, spills from loading and un-loading of tankers, the occasional spectacular accident with massive spills on tens of thousands of tonnes, and the far greater quantities of oil and oil products that find their way from onshore drainage, via waterways to the seas.

The nuclear industry is a source of threats to health, and pollution of the environment, at every stage of the fuel cycle: mining of uranium, processing to "yellow cake", enrichment of uranium, operation of power plants, transport of irradiated waste (with the unavoidable risk of accidents, and its re-processing to yield plutonium, the most dangerous substance of all, which is also transported. Irradiated nuclear waste is regularly transported around the world because countries operating nuclear power stations prefer not to face the insoluble and politically delicate issue of waste disposal. Plants processing uranium yield quantities of plutonium, the smallest grain of which can cause cancer, yet it is transported by the tonne. There is convincing evidence, accumulated over the years, of higher rates of leukaemia, especially among children, in areas round nuclear power stations. "Incidents", as the nuclear industry calls them, are frequent and though played down by the industry inevitably involve risks of irradiation for workers and surrounding population. Accidents may be rare but when they happen there is no limit to the potential disaster. Three Mile Island and Tchernobyl have become household names. But what of the explosion at the waste storage area of Khustum, in the Urals, in 1958, concealed for a decade (though known to western intelligence) and leaving a "no go" area of 50 x 100 km still closed to all habitation ?! What of the "near miss" at the La Hague re-processing plant in northern France, on April 15 1980, when the failure of electricity supply brought the waste cooling system to within minutes of a vast explosion ?! The full and detailed indictment of the nuclear industry would fill a book on its own. The period of out-and-out arms race between east and west has left its legacy of nuclear problems, among them the storage facilities with vast quantities of waste, and the risk of explosions (like that just mentioned). The Hanlon valley re-processing facilities were discovered to have buried thousands of tonnes of highly irradiated material, which was leaking into water supplies in surrounding areas. Among the many cases of irresponsible handling of nuclear material in the Soviet Union, now coming to light, was the dumping into the Sea of Murmansk of used fuel, still highly contaminated, from the miniature reactors in de-commissioned nuclear-powered submarines.

"The frog that nearly died..."

The story bears re-telling of the Chinese teacher and the lesson on evolution.The teacher puts a pan with cold water on the gas, and when it has heated drops in a frog, which immediately jumps out to save its skin. Then he puts the frog in cold water, and heats the pan slowly over the gas: the frog can never make up its mind that the time has come to jump.... What makes this fable relevant is the fact that so many ecological problems are getting progressively worse. The ever-increasing attention paid to ecological issues by the media is in some ways misleading: for awareness does not in itself reduce pollution - it is the very first step towards that goal; and until practical steps begin to be taken, the spread of pollution will continue to expand. The very scale and complexity of the problems imposes time-lags that are depressingly long.   One example will make the point. It concerns a particular aspect of the self-destruction process. In the course of the 1970's, health workers on aid programmes in all corners of the globe began to be increasingly worried about the impact of breast-milk substitutes (better known as "infant formula"). Designed for use in rich countries with running water supplies, and by mothers who can read the instructions and be expected to heed them, they become lethal in the conditions prevailing in developing countries. The powder is diluted with the only water available, frequently a source of infection, and diluted far beyond the level indicated in order to save money. Utensils are not sterilised.The substitute lacks the resistance to disease possessed by breast milk. Ignoring these risks, or just not caring about them, the manufacturers (all multinational companies from Europe or the United States) vie with each other to promote sales, through free samples, and advertising both to medical staff and to the public. A senior United Nations official estimated the number of children dying as a result of breast-milk substitutes at a million a year.

It was to take roughly a decade to develop a world-wide network concerned about the problem (IBFAN International Baby Foods Network - one of the best-organised and most successful non-governmental action networks) and force the problem on the attention of world opinion, and onto the agenda of the World Health Organisation and the United Nations Children's Emergency Fund. For a second period of about ten years,there was a struggle to get something effective done. The industry fought a rearguard battle, insisting that a "voluntary code" of behaviour would be respected by the firms. Only when this had turned out to be fiasco was WHO able to get acceptance for a binding code, which was adopted unanimously (save for one vote: the United States, which voted against because it saw in the WHO code a precedent for the UN monitoring the behaviour of companies). Today, more than a quarter of a century since the alarm was sounded, the struggle continues. Similar stories could be told about many issues. For instance, the fate of the Antarctic, and the time it took to raise the level of public awareness, and to transmute that awareness first into pressure and then into binding international decisions.

A problem only now forcing itself on public awareness is that of the irretrievable destruction of parts of the eco-system which are of a complexity we still cannot comprehend, and a beauty that can never be matched. Nor is this purely an aesthetic issue: only now, too, are we coming to realise the dangers to survival resulting from the impoverishment of the genetic heritage of the eco-sphere, and the folly of destroying areas where there are plants with as yet unexplored healing potential, and humans with the skills to use them.

Water crisis ahead

There is not one crisis about water, but a whole series. Most informed citizens will know of several of them - oil spills and tanker accidents, beaches not safe for bathing, dead lakes and rivers.The "green house effect" is also in fact a problem about water, for the threat that hangs over us derives from the potential impact of a rising sea level on hundreds of the world's cities, built on coasts. But the sense of urgency that has been engendered over this prospect is not matched by any more general concern at our irresponsible attitudes to water.It was in fact the pollution of rivers and the "death" of lakes that inspired the pioneers of the environmental movement, including Rachel Carson with "Silent Spring". To-day the same

14

problem remains unsolved. Indeed, intensive farming, under the pressure of competition, leads to the use of excessive amounts of nitrates, which pollute the water table and endanger supplies of drinking water for towns and cities. It will continue to get worse until the necessary strict rules takes effect against any pollution of either seas or inland waters, and either the necessary purification plants have been built or the methods of production that resulted in the pollution have been modified. As with other aspects of industrial pollution, on land, both legislation and investment will be needed.

Meanwhile, parts of the Mediterranean are so polluted that they would take years to come to life again. The opening up of access to the facts about the Baltic has shown that it was used as a waste tip, with no concern for pollution, by municipalities round its shores, and above all by industry in the former Communist countries. Public attention is caught, and rightly, by the periodic major accidents - Amoco Cadiz, Torrey Canyon, Exxon, Braer...- spilling tens of thousands of tonnes of crude into the sea at one go. They are a reminder of the failure of the international community to enforce precautions that have been recognised for decades as a minimum: for instance, double hulls, which prevent an accident leading to spills. But each big accident also brings its reminder that the quantities involved are limited compared with the total annual pollution of the seas, which comes from spills at boring rigs and during trans-shipment, ships of all flags washing out their bilges at sea (long since an illegal act, but seldom penalised), and oil waste from transport and machinery making its way via rivers and estuaries to the sea. Oil and other waste then finds its way into the food chains, starting with plankton, until birds and sea mammals absorb levels of pollution that are lethal.

The process of destruction is made blatant in the poorest countries. It constitutes a vicious circle, the links in which are indebtedness to the rich world, and knowing but unavoidable destruction of the environment, in some cases on a scale that adds to the immediate threats to the eco-sphere. One of the starting-points is the search by multinational companies for big profits to be had from supplying the consumers of the rich northern countries - the "hamburger syndrome". They buy up land that was previously used to grow subsistence crops for the local population. Instead comes ranching, or highly mechanised mono-culture -maize, bananas - all produced for export. The former small farmers, deprived of their livelihood, drift to the towns. Since they have to be fed, food imports grow. To pay for them means loans, and a burden of interest that grows every year. Those imports add to luxury goods for the local élites, and massive purchases of weaponry - military aircraft come high on the list - which is at best a wasteful badge of national pride, at worse an instrument to repress opposition.Also part of the vicious circle is the way in which the poor, under pressure to survive, are obliged to destroy their own environment (every scrap of wood in the arid areas collected and burned as firewood) or allow it to be destroyed (the obliteration of the rain forests, leaving a thin soil layer that will first serve for ranching, and then within years become eroded, leaving a waste-land.)

The prevailing economic system

The implosion of the communist systems has contributed a new clarity to debate about responsibility for economic and social crises, and for environmental damage. Revelations about the irresponsible approach to industrial pollution in the central and eastern European countries, and throughout the Soviet Union, proved the point that had been made all along by many ecologists: that it was neither capitalism nor communism in itself that led to environmental damage and destruction, but the pressure to produce the most for the lowest cost, that was common to both systems. That there was a difference of degree is to be attributed to the freedom of speech and organisation in the western countries, which led first to a realisation of the dangers from pollution, both in industry and in the environment generally, and then to political pressure to take the necessary steps to reduce it, if need be via legislation. That whole process of democratic control was missing in the Soviet Union and the central and eastern European countries. With the free market emerging as the prevailing economic system world-wide, it will be judged on its merits, no longer on the comparison with the situation in the "other" system.

The essence of the free market system is that any action is justified in terms of economic competition, its success demonstrated by survival, and that in turn dependent upon profit margins and the accumulation of capital. This rule over-rides any notion of solidarity, and any concern for social well-being. The only restrictions are those imposed by binding legislation, by organised labour, or by the pressure of public opinion exerted through the media or by the direct action of groups of citizens. Thus the system encourages the ever-tougher competition which leads to cut-backs in staff and adds to the ranks of the unemployed. If a firm can replace skilled workers on the production line by multi-function robots, thus making several hundred

16

workers redundant, then the system stands for its right to do so, whatever the implications for the workers and their families, or for communities in the area. Governments may seek to promote investment in productive capacity, or boost it with state aids. Such measures are generally presented as creating jobs, though this is less and less often the case; legislation may be adopted that obliges firms to give workers advance notice of sackings, and pay compensation, but there is no government which has a basis for intervening to prevent a firm reducing its workforce.

Such an idea goes to the very roots of the autonomy of employers.In the late '70's the European Commission tabled measures to oblige companies - even multinationals - to give workers' representatives advance notice of investment plans that would have an impact on structures of production and above all on employment. The measure had the support of the trade unions, but it provoked a more virulent reaction from industrialists' organisations and multinationals than anything in the Commission's history. By all-out lobbying of the European Parliament, the opponents succeeded in extracting the teeth from the project, leaving the "Vredeling directive" so watered down that it would not really limit the freedom of action of the big firms, nor give the unions any real new powers

At the origin of the disappearance of crafts, and of traditional skills, lies once again the pressure of ruthless competition. Individual craftsmen cannot compete successfully with furniture, housing, clothes, toys that are mass-produced, using either cheap labour in (or from) the poorer countries, cheap materials, or increasing robotisation.

The role of the multinational companies is far from being clearly understood. It was striking that the Brundtland Report, compiled with goodwill and based on assiduous investigation of the views of national and international experts on development and the environment had a blind spot on precisely that issue. It demonstrated more clearly than any previous report how poverty and environmental destruction interact: but in all its pages there was little more than a paragraph on the multinationals, naively enlisting their support for third world development).

The arms trade provides the clearest demonstration of the extent to which a system of concentrated economic power can outweigh formal political commitments. Fine words about the need to cease supplying weapons to politically unacceptable régimes stand for nothing in the face of the importance of arms exports to the balance of payments. Despite the major initial moves acts of nuclear disarmament carried out by the USA and the former Soviet Union, the chances of a peaceful context in which to affront the challenges of sociological and ecological problems are undermined by the unlimited availability of weaponry of every sort, ranging from nuclear weapons (tactical as well as strategic) and "high tech"weapons capable of causing horrific carnage, to the machine-guns, mortars and snipers' rifles that can turn an incident into a skirmish, and a local shoot-out into the first step towards a civil war.

Thus right across the board, the crises we have identified find their origins in the prevailing economic system, where competition for economic domination and the concentration of economic power justify activities which clash with any notion of human solidarity. When it comes to jobs, profits from investing in robots, or concentrating production, over-rule any notion of concern for the social impact of unemployment on individuals and of regions. Ruthless competition spells the end of craftsmanship and of local communities. Exploitation of the economic potential of poorer areas is at the root of the diabolical circle of indebtedness, impoverishment and ecological destruction. Competition for markets explains the continuance of an arms trade without which the destruction and suffering resulting from local and regional conflicts would be impossible.

This then is the overall crisis of self-destruction. The challenge which faces world society, and more immediately, as we have seen, the emergent European political unit, is to bring about radical change in this situation. That is only to be done through exerting political control over the economic forces that are at the origins of the destruction. With the emergence of powerful economic forces, abusing their strength carelessly to impose inhuman working and living conditions, there was a threefold reaction aimed at imposing checks and balances: the counter-weight of organised labour, with the threat of its withdrawal; the pressure of public opinion; and the resultant introduction of social legislation.

The economic forces operating today at the world level have escaped this kind of control. Their world-wide base gives them the mobility to escape constraints that have remained limited to the national dimension. Labour has failed, for many understandable reasons, to organise to exert its weight effectively at the international level; there is no international public opinion, owing to language and political barriers; and there is as yet no constitutional framework within which control can be exerted through legislation. The challenge thus turns out to be essentially political. It must involve building up effective institutions, with genuine democratic legitimacy, in order to exert political control. At the same time, there will be a need for a radical change in prevailing values, with competition, the profit motive and the free market seen for what they are: forces which must be brought under control.

We are all taking part, knowingly or not, in a race between the forces of auto-destruction, and those who are committed to a radically different vision of relations between people, and people's place and responsibilities in the eco-sphere. The first step, of awareness, progresses apace: but the identification and promotion of alternative policies, the recruiting of democratically organised support, and finally the establishment of the institutions needed to carry the policies through - for these there seem today to be only meagre grounds for hope.

Against this background of crisis, and this range of challenges, the Europeans have to react, in their own interests and in that of the planet. For decades they have failed to recognise the responsibilities that go with the power that they seek to wield. They have continued to be caught up in paralysing and pointless struggles, while new problems emerged around them. Before going on to a critical analysis of their detailed track record, and the forces which have so far won out, we must seek to understand the reasons for the massive failure of the last four decades.

2 The European failure

The way the Europeans react to the challenge of so many inter-locking crises could be decisive, for themselves and for the rest of the world. The European Community is already the world's biggest trading and economic unit, and destined to become even stronger as all other European states become linked to it. An effective European federation, pooling the political weight and experience of the European countries, could not avoid playing a major role on all major issues. But if an internal tug-of-war over institutions should remain the over-riding concern of key European governments - the UK above all - then there can be no effective European reaction to the challenges of the next few years

Inevitably, it is the European Union and the European Community which will provide the hard core of whatever new institutional arrangement emerges in Europe. But measured against their potential, the track record of the Europeans is not encouraging. Despite the aura of success that the Community has generated, it turns out on closer inspection to be one of the great failures of history - the well-meant efforts of several generations of convinced "Europeans" notwithstanding. Statesmen and governments, though formally committed to European unity, have proved incapable of drawing on Europe's wealth of political and constitutional experience to create a viable political unit. So nearly half a century of efforts to have "Europe" speak with one voice in world affairs - let alone act together in crisis situations - have led only to the humiliating incapacity to act demonstrated in the fiasco over the disintegration of Yugoslavia.

For decades, the Europeans have sat on their increasingly prosperous hams, in an oasis of well-being, paying lip-service to the goal of a united Europe, but missing the chances that history was offering them. As an island of conflict-free prosperity (save for local confrontations in Ireland, the Basque

21

country and Corsica), they had the chance gradually to develop the necessary experience of reacting together to outside challenges: they failed to take it. One of the myths is that they have reached their targets, and that the unification process has been an historic achievement and a model to be copied in other regions of the world.The reality is less shiny.

True, the western European countries have enjoyed decades of prosperity, stimulated in part by the freeing of trade; but the removal of customs barriers was not special to the Community, it covered the whole of western Europe. The more demanding target of a genuine "common market" with no economic barriers at all was neglected, to be resuscitated 25 years behind schedule...when big industry discovered it would be in its interest.True, too, the threat of war between European countries was eliminated - in part because war is inconceivable between countries whose economies, after decades of integration, are so deeply interdependent. But the era of peace in Europe as a whole owed more to the military deadlock between the United States and the Soviet Union than to the uniting of western Europe.

One of the dreams of the founders of the Community had been of Europe with an influential voice in world affairs. When the ideological log-jam broke, at the end of the '80s, and unpredictable conflicts flared up, they revealed that the western Europeans had wasted four decades. They could have put the years of peace and prosperity to good use to equip themselves with the necessary institutions to react - rapidly, effectively and as a unit - to any challenge and above all to any threat to peace, whether within Europe or outside.

Instead, the European Community/Union has got itself into a situation where it has to try to react simultaneously to three kinds of challenge. It has to elaborate policies covering the whole gamut from security in eastern and central Europe to trade relations with the USA and Japan, and to planetary issues like third world indebtedness and pending ecological disaster. It has also to adapt to a change in its own dimensions as the remaining rich western European countries seek membership, and the rest of Europe wants involvement with the promise of membership on the not too distant horizon. Finally, it needs to develop viable institutions to enable it to act as a unit, and to exert genuine democratic control.

In a world that continues to shrink, thanks to developments in communications technology, and where federal states have been wrought apart by resurgent nationalisms - the Soviet Union, Yugoslavia, Czechoslovakia...- the Maastricht Treaty looks like a belated bid to run against the tide, putting together a super-state. There is in fact a double battle

22

to be fought out, to determine how the Europeans will work together. Built into the text of the Maastricht Treaty are the two existing options - the "Community" approach (being used for economic and social issues), and the inter-governmental approach (for home affairs, foreign policy and defence). But there is a second pair of alternatives: continuation of the present mixed formula with its built-in tensions and limitations; or the establishment of a decentralised federal formula which empowers its institutions to act effectively, but ensures effective democratic control.

Four decades in perspective

To assess what kind of federation, with what priorities, is the most likely to emerge, it is necessary to get the efforts and the failures of the past four decades into historical perspective. As with any long-established political unit there are solidly rooted practices, and the usual complex mesh of vested interests.

The first attempts at unity began in the early years after the end of the Second World War, as soon as the basic structures of government were working again, and the necessities of life ensured. Many in the resistance and in the prisoner-of-war camps had dreamed of a united federal Europe rising from the ashes of the old system of national rivalries, as a guarantee that such a war should not recur. The draft manifesto, written in 1941-2 in a fascist detainment camp on the island of Ventotene by Altiero Spinelli and Ernesto Rossi, sketched the outlines of a united Europe. But the "federalists" were not to find it easy to put their ideas into practice. Perhaps inevitably, the starting-point for re-building, be it of cities or of political systems, was to be the nation states as they had existed before the war.

With a sound federal reflex, the United States made the Marshall Plan, through which it provided vital aid for re-construction, conditional upon the countries that were going to benefit coordinating their policies. The Organisation for European Economic Cooperation fulfilled that function as far as economic policy was concerned, but the political reality was another matter: a patchwork of states had moved in to fill the institutional vacuum. Before the end of the '40s, the ideological division of Europe had become a reality: east and west would seek their own forms of integration.

The first political initiative for unity was the Council of Europe, encompassing all the democratic western European countries. It had both a parliamentary assembly (purely consultative, with delegates from national parliaments) and a committee of ministers (with no power to make or apply policies).

On the face of it the Council of Europe failed because there were deep-rooted divergences in the attitudes of the various countries towards unification. On the one side were the continental countries that had seen the structures of society and of the state, as well as their towns, cities and infrastructure, rased to the ground, and were profoundly committed to ensuring that it could not happen again. On the other were the northern countries that had not known occupation or the collapse of society. Winston Churchill's speech in Zurich on Sept.19 1946, making it clear that Britain did not see itself as an integral part of a unified Europe, but as a benevolent outsider, has been quoted to death to illustrate an attitude that has motivated United Kingdom policy throughout the period. The Nordic countries, too (neutrals or not) were totally unprepared to get involved in a pooling of sovereignty. But it can be argued that the real political gap lay not between countries with differing approaches, but between the nation state "establishments" and those involved in the effort to create a united Europe.

With the Council of Europe still-born, the drive came for a core group of six countries to "go it alone". The idea for a new approach came from Jean Monnet, with his unique record of creative initiatives for international cooperation. He was convinced from long personal experience that for countries to work effectively together, there needed to be an institution at the centre with a mandate to help them agree on what was best in their joint interest.

To show the effectiveness of the approach, he proposed testing it in the key sector of the coal and steel industries: if they could be mingled, by removing all barriers and installing a central authority, war between the countries concerned would become impossible. For the French the plan promised a lasting guarantee against renewed German aggression; for the Germans it offered involvement on a footing of equality. The result was the Coal and Steel Community. The principal innovation was the High Authority, with direct powers to regulate the two sectors.

The success of the Coal and Steel Community encouraged the governments of the Six to aim higher and further. Plans were drawn up for a defence community, and for a political community, and were welcomed in all the countries involved. What was not predicted was the paradoxical alliance that came into being in France between the Gaullists, opposed to what they saw as a surrender of national sovereignty, and the Communists, against what they saw as an emergent military power with all the combined force of

Germany and France. The defence community plan was voted down in the French National Assembly, and the political union project was buried with it, not to be unearthed for three decades.

The forces in the Six working for integration still had the drive for one more effort. They fell back on economic integration. Monnet justified this on the grounds that once economic ties had resulted in a sense of common destiny, the way would be open for political unity. But the governments had not appreciated the experience of the High Authority, which escaped their control, and when it came to negotiating the European Economic Community, the Monnet formula was watered down. The central body independent of the governments and responsible for the good of the Community as a whole was retained: the Commission. But it was not to have any of the direct powers possessed by the High Authority. Instead, it would draft proposals for the application of the Treaty, and have the right of initiative; but the decisions would be taken by the Council of Ministers (one minister per country), with a system of weighted voting. A move to majority voting was provided for, at the end of eight years, and it was over an attempt to have that commitment abandoned that de Gaulle, now President of France with untramelled responsibility for external policy, clashed head-on with his partners in 1966.

De Gaulle versus the Five

The President of the Commission, former German under-secretary Walter Hallstein, had infuriated de Gaulle by acting as as though he were a head of state, giving visitors from all over the world the red carpet treatment. More fundamental was de Gaulle's realisation that the introduction of majority voting in the Council, due in January 1967, would infringe French national sovereignty. The Five resisted a French boycott, with the Germans in particular determined not to breach an international Treaty; and with French farmers not prepared to see their subsidies from the Common Farm Policy budget put at risk, de Gaulle had to climb down. But majority voting became a taboo, and any progress towards a more federal way of operating was headed off.

The early years of the Common Market gave those involved a sense of making historical progress: the removal of customs duties; the Community speaking with one voice in international trade negotiations; the establishment, under dramatic circumstances, of the Common Agricultural Policy...all were

25

indeed achievements.

In the mid-'70s and early '80s the Community began to lose its momentum. But this was partly masked by events, in particular the enlargement of the Community, first to Denmark, Ireland and the United Kingdom, and then to Greece and to Spain and Portugal when democracy in those countries was restored. There were other seemingly important steps. The heads of government began to be directly involved in the affairs of the Community, holding regular "summit" meetings of the French President and the heads of government of the other eleven countries, with the President of the Commission grudgingly admitted. The Community foreign ministers began to move cautiously into the field of foreign policy: they met not as the EEC Council but "in political cooperation" outside the terms of the Treaties. Then they started edging into the field of security policy. In 1979 the Assembly, made up of delegates from the national parliaments, which had never had more than a consultative role, was replaced by a European Parliament to be directly elected every five years.

The Parliament predictably set out to claim more powers for itself - but within the framework of the Community system as it existed. It sought above all to claw back from the Council of Ministers some of the power of decision over the Community budget. But an early trial of strength led to a deadlock which left the Community languishing without funds through until the autumn of the following year, when the prospect of protests by angry farmers drove the two institutions to a compromise. The Parliament had to face the bitter fact that it had not got a better deal in the summer than it would have done in December. There was no better reminder that the nation states had not intended to reinforce democratic control over the Community.

The institutional tug-o'-war

What has been going on over the past decades has been a sort of institutional tug-of-war, with the Commission (generally backed by the Parliament) seeking to affirm its position, and the member States seeking to avoid ceding sovereignty to the Community institutions. This has left the Community in a sort of constitutional no-man's-land, neither a purely inter-governmental organisation with an a-political secretariat, nor the beginnings of a federal European state.

If after four decades of talk about a world role the Community is still not equipped to speak with one voice, and less capable of acting decisively as a unit, then there is little doubt about where the responsibility lies: with the "medium-sized powers" France and Britain. It is there that the governing élite still sees its country as carrying weight in the affairs of the world, separately from the Community, as well as playing a leading role in Community affairs. The British war with Argentina over the Malvinas, and frequent French military interventions in Tchad, the Congo, Gabon and elsewhere have confirmed their readiness to use their military capacity autonomously, outside the Community or the United Nations framework. The French are deadly serious about their role and responsibilities in the southern hemisphere, where Tahiti, New Caledonia and Réunion are thought of not as colonies but as part of France.

The decisions to be taken or the policies to be followed in the Community institutions are treated as being just one part of foreign policy. Were it not for France previously and the United Kingdom since it joined, there could probably have begun to be a cautious move towards a common foreign policy, and perhaps even a reform of the Institutions, based on a federal approach. But what France and Britain totally lack is any grasp of the meaning and practice of federalism. Historically, this is understandable: the story of both these nations is of a centralised state gradually extending its control, and with a record of several hundred years of autonomous (colonial and neo-colonial) intervention on the world. This is in stark contrast to the position of Germany, Italy or France, all of which have developed on a federal model. It is natural for those who have come of age politically in a federal context to understand the need for a federal level in the affairs of the Community. Belgium shares this understanding. Other member countries - the Netherlands, Denmark, Portugal, Ireland, Luxembourg - are centralised, but acutely aware of how little influence they can wield in world affairs save via the Community. Joseph Luns, for long years Dutch foreign minister, when asked why such a small country needed two ministers dealing with international matters, replied: " When you are so small, the rest of the world looks far bigger.." The smaller countries are also aware that they have little to expect from an inter-governmental system, where the big countries inevitably call the tune. The attachment of the Benelux countries to the European Community formula, with its weighted majority voting is based on experience. But it will almost certainly be taken over by the relatively small countries now likely to join, none of which will join the European Union to be told what to do by the bigger partners. A federal system would certainly have the support of most of the smaller countries.

Past experience shows that peaceful change in a political system can take place according to one of two possible scenarios. In the first, the goal is to bring about change - change which may be urgent and radical, or seen as a process of long-term reform - within an existing institutional context. This, for instance, is the approach of socialist or social-democratic parties whose target is (or was...) to introduce socialism in their own particular country.

The other scenario is one in which the political class in a country perceives a need to adapt to a changed political dimension, precisely as a condition for preserving its shared basic values. This was the situation at the stage in American history when the states of the north came together. It was also one aspect of the European situation as perceived by the "founding fathers" of the European Community - Jean Monnet and the christian-democrat leaders who shared his approach. They wanted Europe to play a world role. They also wanted a western Europe strong enough to defend itself against the Communist threat from the East. But in accepting the need to create a bigger western European unit, they were not concerned to bring about political change: their goal was to strengthen and maintain the existing system, the "soft liberalism" of the post-war period. (It could probably be argued that the Rome Treaty, creating the Economic Community, was less a founding charter for uniting Europe - which was left as a vaguely-defined goal - than a reflection of the concerns and priorities of the liberal system which they were keen to underpin by working closely together. Whence, perhaps, the striking lack of any broad vision of that role on the world scene which the first wave of federalists had seen as one of their over-riding goals.

So on the face of it the efforts to unite Europe were radical as regards the framework, and conservative as far as society was concerned. But the practice of nearly four decades was to reveal the strength of the conservative reflex, above all among national administrations and political establishments, when it came to envisaging a new "federal" dimension. The reason is not hard to find: politics, the civil service, journalism are all careers where the top of the pyramid lies within the national framework. To introduce a new level "above their heads" would be to downgrade the status and the power (or illusion of power) of precisely those in a position to further or to delay the unification process. This fundamental clash is more acute in the case of France and the United Kingdom. The movement to unite Europe has thus turned out to be doubly conservative. The new impetus given it at the end of the '80s, at the instigation of economic forces and with the acquiescence of the governments, replaced the mild liberalism of the Community's founding principles by a mercantile approach reflecting the aggressive "Euro-Thatcherism" prevailing in the member states. Strikingly, the "free market" principle was written into the Maastricht Treaty. In the European Commission, the committed socialist Delors has fought in vain to obtain a dynamic EC social policy, whereas his arch-privatiser colleague, Sir Leon Brittan, has ridden with the tide of government support.

At the institutional level, the negotiations leading to the Maastricht Treaty involved mock struggles between the advocates of two versions of the existing system - one with the Community element reinforced, as Delors would have wished; the other clearly inter-governmental in inspiration. There was no real debate about federalism, because it was not even on the agenda.

So as the European Union comes face to face with the pressing need for a foreign policy, its leaders have not so much as explored what kind of institutional system will be needed to achieve such a policy. To make things worse, the political context in which they have to operate has changed profoundly. The long post-war period of stagnation in the national political systems has given way to changes on a scale and taking place at a pace never seen before. The players projected into the "Europe Game" - whether as national ministers or as members of the European Parliament, will not be the same. They will be defending different priorities. Above all, many of them will not share the basic uncritical commitment to European unity that guaranteed a consensus over the past four decades. A brief overview of the political scene in some of the key countries will illustrate the kind of changes that are happening, and provide part of the context for the next few years.

3 Political mosaic

Most aspects of life in modern society have become internationalised. Sport has gone furthest: politics the least far.TV enables those who are interested to follow between 20 and 30 sports. Fans and supporters know the names of the leading teams and the top stars world-wide, and are prepared to follow them to the ends of the earth - or as far as international charter flights will allow. Tens of millions all over the world watch the Olympics round the clock. Clothing has gone the same way: jeans, T-shirts and sneakers are the symbols of a world-wide cultural area ("civilisation"...?) with fashions and styles of dress rapidly becoming uniform. Food, alas, is under similar pressure, with local customs and styles gradually losing out in the struggle with the merchants of "quick", industrial food. The privately-owned automobile, household equipment, and a vast range of consumer goods have imposed a life-style that has spread around the globe. New communications technology has meant that a single planetary audience is told the same news - the same selection of what has happened in the world, with the same underlying ideological and commercial message.

The one major exception to the onward march of uniformity has been politics. It continues to take place in isolation, rendered inaccessible by the barriers of language. The exceptions are those rare occasions when there is a major political upheaval or a local conflict. For most of the time ordinary citizens, if they are interested in politics at all, follow what is going on in their own country, and feel unaffected by political events in countries that may be geographically quite near, but remain culturally and politically remote.Now the dual technologies of space and telecommunications are opening up a new development: the world-wide market in news, (as seen and edited, of course, in Washington or Atlanta), which gradually fosters a sense of common identity amongst those who watch or listen. Given the complexity of the flood of information, it is rare that national news makes it to the international headlines.

Events occurring at the level of the European Community are more remote than those in neighbouring European countries: they might as well have been taking place on a magic carpet, or on another planet. The concerned citizen cannot fit them into a familiar context, as he or she can with national or local stories. So it is only occasionally that decisions or developments in the Community institutions are felt by the ordinary citizen to be impinging on his or her everyday life One exception is when the farmers converge on Brussels to demonstrate about prices: they are almost the only group whose income - and for many, their survival - is effectively determined by decisions (usually against their interests) taken by the ministers and their attendant Eurocrats, in a remote sixth storey conference room in Brussels. A revealing case occurred in 1993 when the international trade talks (which in the past had remained the preserve of experts) aroused with surprising rapidity the interest of the international media. Not the least of the reasons for this was an all-out campaign by the United States to get its views across, and put the Community on the defensive.

Being partners in the Community has not led to a better knowledge or understanding, on the part of public opinion, of events on the domestic scene in other EC countries. Only those in the Community institutions involved in working out compromises acceptable to all, and the journalists following their doings, have been forced to understand what were the domestic political pressures behind the negotiating positions of their Community partners. For the policies of the Community are in reality a reflection of the national realities that have to be taken into account in order to reach agreement.

Tomorrow, if a federal system of some kind gradually comes into being, the concerned and well-informed citizen is going to have to develop a higher level of acquaintance than is the case today with political life in at least the key European countries among the 12, 17, or one day even 30 or more member states.

The politics of the European countries constitute an extraordinarily complex mosaic, reflecting in each case the course of their domestic history, their electoral system and the institutional patterns for which they have opted. A thousand years of history as a centralised state results in deep-rooted attitudes very different from those prevailing in countries with a federal tradition that came into being in the last century, or those whose statehood dates from only decades ago. An electoral system with far-reaching proportional representation yields a different kind of politics from a system of single-member constituencies. Most obvious of all, a prime minister dependent on a narrow parliamentary majority is in a very different position from a directly-elected president certain of several years more in office. But a prime minister with an absolute majority can discount opposition from the within his/her party, and rule effectively as a "democratic dictator".

Throughout the post-World War period, politics in western Europe was marked by a high degree of stability: shifts of opinion were often reflected by changes of a few percentage points in the scores of the parties. Initially this stagnation, as it might better be called, was due to the outside pressures of the "cold war". Later, it was seen as a sound political basis for the years of successful growth.

But with the fall of the Berlin Wall, the end of east-west confrontation, and the example of upheavals in the eastern European countries, the constraints were released. After a pause as public opinion reacted to the new situation, the log-jam began to break (and for once the image was an apposite one). The electors no longer felt responsible for political stability: on the contrary, they sought to express a long-dammed-up desire for change, and welcomed the chance to express their dissatisfaction with the lack of imagination, the corruption, and the remoteness from the citizen which had marked the politics of the preceding decades.

The result has been a series of upheavals on a scale never thought to be possible, and affecting, in different ways, the political scene in many of the key European countries. Most dramatic of all have been the events in Italy, with the virtual disappearance of the Christian-Democrat party that had ruled continuously throughout the post-war period. France saw an unprecedented swing of electoral support from the party in power (the socialists) to the opposition; and in the Netherlands the swing away from the Labour party has been such that it cannot hope to rule in the foreseeable future without an alliance with the christian-democrats. Several countries - Germany, Belgium, Italy, France - face the emergence of racist or extreme right parties taking a serious share of the vote.

What follows here is an attempt to sketch the political scene in some of the key countries.It offers the kind of basic knowledge that should help readers to put political events in the countries concerned into an intelligible framework. It is based on an acquaintance with the politics of the different countries, acquired over several decades, knowledge of the languages, and on-going political and personal contacts.

Germany: anchor under stress

Germany is almost the only genuinely federal state not just in the European Community but also, since the collapse of Yugoslavia and the separation of the Czech Republic and Slovakia, in the whole of Europe. There is an active political life at the level of the regions (Lände) - some of which, like Nord-Rhein Westfalen or Bavaria, have populations and economies to match those of states like Belgium or the Netherlands. In the civil service or in politics, it is possible to make a satisfying career in a region - or to opt for the federal level.

Drafted after World War II, the federal constitution was specifically intended to avoid pitfalls into which Germany had fallen in the past. The electoral system is based on a combination of regionally-based members and others elected proportionally on national lists, a formula that tends to nurture a system with two main parties, but allow space for small parties alongside them, able sometimes to tip the parliamentary balance. A key measure has been the 5% threshold, which any party must pass if it to win any seats at all. Reflecting the trauma of the Weimar Republic in the 1920's, this was a precaution intended to prevent minor extremist parties getting a foothold from which they could sabotage the parliamentary system. Each party chooses a candidate - who is not necessarily the party leader - to compete for the post of "Chancellor" (prime minister) at the next elections. If a Chancellor in office loses the confidence of the Parliament, it does not automatically mean early elections: there is an obligation on the party challenging the incumbent to try to form an alternative government on the base of a new coalition within the parliament. The time-table for elections in the regions is entirely autonomous, providing several times a year a test of trends in voters' attitudes. The balance of support in the regions is reflected in the upper chamber, the Federal Council (Bundesrat). That is an on-going body made up of representatives of the regions, and if the results of regional elections cause the majority in the Bundesrat to swing against the government, it operates as a warning against proposing controversial measures. Taken together, these precautions have yielded a political system that is stable but at the same time lively enough to retain citizens' interest and involvement. Thanks to regional politics, there is not the sense of remoteness from the citizens which is strongly felt in some countries.

Only after a historic conference at Bad Godesberg, where it renounced the notion of class struggle and opted for a reformist line, did the social-democratic party become eligible for government. That ushered in a period in the '50s and '60s when power lay with the "Big Coalition" of Christian-Democrats and Social-Democrats. Then the Christian-Democrats governed with the support of the Liberals. Later it was the Liberals who switched partners, and began what was to be a long political partnership with the Social Democrats. The '90's started with the Christian-Democrats back in power allied with the Liberals. Though at times they only just scraped over the 5% hurdle at the federal level, the Liberals have exerted an influence out of all proportion to their numbers, in the country or in Parliament. Their leader, Hans Genscher, was the Federal Republic's foreign minister for over a decade, becoming the senior foreign minister of the Twelve. The Liberals also insisted on holding the post of minister of finance.

The Federal Republic was the first European country where a "green" party succeeding in breaking into national politics. In 1978 the Greens slipped over the 5% bar, which gave them 27 seats in the Bundestag. They were returned again but having wasted much popular good will by public displays of their own disunity, both ideological and personal, in 1990 they misjudged the mood of the electorate over unification, and failed to get the vital 5%. This has not stopped them continuing to do well in some regional elections, and even taking part in coalition governments in several regions.

Federal Germany has not only been a model of political balance and stability. It has also been - and the two are not unrelated - a model of economic stability. Several factors contributed to this. One was the fundamental agreement of trade unions, employers and government on the absolute need for stable prosperity - not least as a guarantee for the democratic system. Another was the role of the Federal Bank ("Bundesbank"), enjoying total independence from the government, and with an obligation written into its statutes to give priority to monetary stability. It is monetary stability, inflation always well under control, and responsible attitudes on the part of the unions, that have given German industry the base it needed for becoming the main supplier, in the engineering and capital goods sectors, for a hinterland covering the whole of western Europe and beyond.

For Germany, the economic and political scene has been overturned by reunification. The way that reunification was carried off was certainly one of the most remarkable episodes in the European history of the past few decades. But it can also be argued that the way it was handled was the first major error by a Federal German government. When the communist régimes in central and eastern Europe began to fall like dominoes, no-one predicted how far or how fast things would go in the German Democratic Republic

(DDR). The initial demonstrations, organised by dissidents who had challenged the old régime, were not in favour of immediate reunification. Nor were the politicians in the west. But both were overtaken by a wave of popular pressure. Once the wall had been first opened, then breached and physically destroyed, Chancellor Kohl saw that he held the trumps, provided he acted fast. Kohl rightly felt that reunification was a matter for the Germans. There could be no question of the "four powers" - the USA, the Soviet Union, Britain and France, victors of the war over four decades earlier - doing anything but acquiesce. A long negotiation would give time for international controversy, of the kind always aroused in the past by any talk of reunification.

Inside Germany, too, Kohl opted to go it alone. It was in many ways a pity that he made no offer to the SPD to deal with reunification together as a matter of national interest. But Kohl's position was precisely that this was a matter of domestic German politics. The magic wand he needed to bring about reunification was at hand: a clause in the Federal German constitution, under which any new region (_Land_) could ask to be admitted to the Federation. With the full agreement of its interim government the DDR was transformed into five new Lände, which at once applied to become part of the German Federal Republic. The parliament that had been elected in the DDR was dissolved, and elections held throughout Germany.

Leaving no trace

In this way the other German state disappeared, legally and constitutionally. Kohl's government then set about ensuring that, as with the Wall, there should be no trace left. There was no thought of sitting down together, to see what there was about the DDR system that might be worth preserving or adapting. There was no question of transition periods, to enable the people of the five new regions to come to terms with their new status. This operation revealed to what an extent the right in the Federal Republic had looked on the DDR as their ideological enemies. To observers from outside, it seemed strange after all the years when the right had attacked the DDR as repressive - implying that its citizens were victims - that these same repressed citizens should be treated as though they were the culprits, collectively responsible for all that was bad in the former East Germany.

In the first Federal elections after unification, the Party for Democratic Socialism - PDS (renovated and rejuvenated successor to the old communist

Social Unity party - SED), benefitted from the concession that parties in the east had only to pass the 5% threshold in the five new regions. In the Federal elections, set for the autumn of 1994, the PDS faced the challenge of achieving the 5% country-wide, which requires around 21% in the five regions. With a growing wave of resentment in the former DDR, above all about unemployment and economic policy, they saw that target as being just possible. For the "Ossie's" (East Germans) the results of Kohl's precipitation are all around them, and can be measured in economic and social terms. During the negotiations on the unification, he had over-ridden the Federal Bank - always supposed to be independent of political interference - to insist on merging the two D-Marks at a 1:1 ratio, as the east Germans wanted, not 2:1 as the Bank recommended. This raised enormously the burden on the west German economy, which at the same time was having to accept commitments in all directions. It had to pay unemployment benefits, previously unknown in the eastern regions. It had to invest on a massive scale in the five new regions, to provide the infrastructure for a programme of economic recovery, which it was hoped would be financed by western capital buying up the key privatised morsels of the DDR economy. It had to contribute, as part of the European Community - the funds urgently needed for the revival of the Russian economy.

Thus the new, bigger, united Germany, rich though it is, solid though it's economy still is, has found itself under enormous economic strain - coming also when it was committed to persuading its EC partners to launch the planned "economic and monetary union.The economic hardship of people in the five new regions is a high price for their new citizenship. Total privatisation means that many outdated firms find no buyers, and will be shut down leaving people with no prospect of jobs; as for the firms taken over by western investors or entrepreneurs, their main concern will be efficiency and high productivity, which as western European workers know spells unemployment for many. The shock is the greater because unemployment was unknown in the DDR, as it was throughout the communist system.

The social and psychological dimensions of the impact of unification are hard to measure. The irrational but understandable surge towards unification brought together in a sort of political shot-gun marriage two peoples who after 40 years had come to have very different attitudes to life, and different codes of behaviour. Add to this the fear of the "Wessies" (Westerners) that the "Ossies" (Easterners) will take their jobs, and the resentment of the Ossies at the level of unemployment, and you have a recipe for friction and frustration for a long time to come. To this must be added the emergence of racist groups and parties, prepared to make immigrant workers and their families the scape-goats for economic disasters.

France: a very presidential democracy

The current French constitution bears the imprint of the powerful personality of de Gaulle. But the political system also reflects a far older tradition of a state having at its centre a figure - once a monarch, more recently a president - who is the personification of France, and acts as such. The Constitution of the Fourth Republic, as it is officially known, combines an elected president, with sole responsibility for foreign policy and defence, and a traditional parliamentary system governing domestic affairs.

What is peculiar about it is the relationship between president and prime minister. The president appoints the prime minister, subject only to the condition that the politician of his choice must be able to win a majority in the Assembly. There is no obligation on the president, in making his choice, to take account of the views of the party whose support won him the presidency. The president can also dismiss the prime minister, at any time, without being required to give any explanation. Thus prime ministers may be dismissed for tactical reasons, even if their policies are widely perceived as being successful and have broad backing amongst the population. That was what happened to the socialist Michel Rocard: he was patently the best choice for prime minister when the socialists won both presidential and legislative elections in 1988, but Mitterrand dismissed him arbitrarily, with no public explanation, at a moment when he was scoring high in the popularity polls. Thus prime ministers are "expendable": Mitterrand appointed eight in all in the first 12 years of his two presidential mandates, due to total 14 years.

The position of prime minister is never a comfortable one. The prime minister designate draws up a list of ministers, but this has to be submitted to the president for approval - which is not always forthcoming. The prime minister also submits a governmental programme, when seeking the investiture of the Assembly, but must take care not to stray into the areas of foreign policy and defence, reserved for the President. Most peculiar of all is the fact that it is the president, not the prime minister, who presides the weekly meetings of the cabinet. The delicate issue of who is to tell the world what the government has decided is solved by having a spokesperson with full ministerial status as a member of the government.

The highly personalised nature of the presidency means that all the main political leaders see being president, not prime minister, as their ultimate goal. To achieve it, they need in general to retain the support of a major party. But with the president elected, like the members of parliament, on a two-round system, would-be candidates must take care to appeal to the centre votes that they will need to swing the second-round result. Although in theory an outsider could run and win, in practice it is candidates with the backing of one of the main parties who have won.

The system has turned out to have some complex side-effects, not foreseen by those who drafted it - above all because of the over-lapping time-tables for the mandates of the president and of the Assembly. The members of the Assembly are elected for four years, the president for seven. But if the successful presidential candidate is from a different political majority, he can dismiss the assembly, and count on new legislative elections to produce an assembly which will back the policies his government stands for. However, it can also happen that opinion in the country swings at parliamentary elections during the course of a presidential mandate. The president then finds himself facing a hostile majority, and with no other course - unless he should choose to resign - than to appoint a prime minister from within that majority. This situation is known to the French as "co-habitation". Thus it was that after a victory of the right in the legislative elections in 1985, the president, François Mitterrand, appointed Jacques Chirac, undisputed leader of the right, as prime minister. The two were not only political rivals, they felt little sympathy for each other. Mitterrand used his political skills in exploiting to the maximum the margin allowed him by the constitution to intervene on a wide range of policy. The next presidential election, two years later, saw him win a renewed majority, which was confirmed when he called legislative elections which the socialists won easily. The co-habitation scenario was repeated in March 1993, when the right won the legislative elections by an overwhelming majority. This time Mitterrand chose neither of the two competing leaders of the right (ex-president Giscard d'Estaing or ex-prime minister Chirac). He appointed Edouard Balladur, a former businessman whom both leaders could accept, and who had not been known to harbour presidential ambitions. It turned out that Mitterrand and Balladur were able to "co-habit" amicably, without visible stress or conflict. Mitterrand, as a lame duck president, approaching the end of a 14-year period in office, knew the limits of his position, especially in the aftermath of the landslide victory of the right. Balladur achieved an unprecedented level of popularity, based more on personality than on policies, and this made him a clear contender for the coveted position as the right's candidate for the presidency.

The break-down whereby the president handles foreign affairs and the prime minister domestic issues resulted for some time in a very special situation as regards the European Community. It is the president who represents France in the regular "summit" meetings of the European Council. He is advised by the foreign minister and other specialised ministers. But Mitterrand frequently left the prime minister (not only Chirac but socialist prime ministers too) to kick his (or her) heels in Paris. In 1993, however, Mitterrand (perhaps to aggravate Giscard and Chirac) took Balladur with him to the summits.

The party system in France, fairly rigid for decades, is undergoing some radical changes. In 1993 the Socialists, leading force on the left since Mitterrand painstakingly welded them together in the 70's, suffered the biggest defeat ever recorded in a French election. The other left party, the Communists, have been in steady decline, from over 20% to less than 10%. The retirement of secretary-general Georges Marchais will end at last a period of anachronistic centralist domination, out of touch with the shake-up in almost all other CPs round the world.

On the right there have been two competing parties, with very different backgrounds and traditions. One is the RPR ("Rassemblement pour la République"), heirs to the Gaullist tradition, deeply attached to French sovereignty and France's world role, and with widespread popular support amongst farmers and workers. It is led by Jacques Chirac, who has been prime minister prime minister twice but also failed in two bids to become president. The other is the UDR ("Union pour la Démocratie Française"),the party of big farmers, land-owners, industrialists and the liberal professions; it is currently led by the former president, Valéry Giscard d'Estaing. Attempts to merge them into a single right-wing party have failed, but the voting system forces them to help each other out by allowing the best placed candidates to win in the second round vote. With neither Giscard nor Chirac prepared to cede to the other, there is now talk of American-style "primaries" to choose a single candidate for the presidential elections. Balladur, on the basis of his current popularity, would run away with the nomination, and perhaps with the presidency.

By contrast with most other European socialist or social-democrat parties, the French socialist party has no deep roots in the working class. As cobbled together by Mitterrand, it has been a party of "notables" - leading figures in local communities - and has always suffered from a surfeit of would-be leaders. By contrast, the Communist party has roots that go deep, and draw on memories of the Popular Front sweeping to power in the '30s, the Resistance, where the Communists provided the hard core, and of tough industrial struggles in the post-war years. But its resilience, and the loyalty it has inspired among workers and intellectuals, have not been matched by the ability to adapt to a changing world. The PCF remained loyal to the Moscow line until there was no Moscow line left to be loyal to. France is the country where the extreme right is the best organised and the most dynamic. The National Front has a leader, Jean-Marie LePen, with the skills to exploit to the full the wave of racism against migrants and first-generation citizens ("beurs") to win votes. He has also been successful in using his voting score to entice those in the right-wing parties who are prepared to do deals with the National Front at the regional or local level.

There have been repeated but largely unavailing efforts to build up a "green" party in France (Cf chapter on "greenery").

Italy: political earthquake

In less than two years, the christian-democrat party that dominated Italian politics since World War II has crumbled, followed by most of the other parties, as revelations of corruption shattered the credibility of the Italian political world.

Throughout the four decades after the Second World War, the pattern of Italian politics remained rigid and unchanging. Like Don Camillo and Pepe, Christian-Democrats and Communists faced it out. The Communists, despite their impeccable record of courage and sacrifice under fascism, their leading role in the resistance against the Germans, their moderation and responsibility in governing the "red" regions of Emilia-Romagna, Tuscany and Umbria, and their tried and tested loyalty to NATO, were relegated permanently to opposition at the national level. That was the joint edict of the United States government, via the American ambassador in Rome and the Vatican. The Communists tried everything to prove their aptitude, with their most charismatic leader, Enrico Berlinguer, convincing his party of the need for an "historic opening": but the ban remained. The most lucid and open-minded of the Christian-Democratic leaders, Aldo Moro, tried to move his party towards accepting the Communists as partners in government - and paid with his life, kidnapped and finally assassinated by some of those (whether extreme left terrorists or extreme right provocateurs has never been clear)

41

who wanted things to stay unchanged.

The rest of the political spectrum also changed little. Immediately to the right of the Communists, the small and insignificant Socialist Party was taken over by a forceful figure, Bettino Craxi, to whom personal ambition mattered more than socialist principles. In the centre of the spectrum were the Social-Democrats, Liberals, and Republicans, small parties who provided the Christian-Democrats with the parliamentary support they needed to stay in power. A similar deal even brought Craxi the coveted post of prime minister, but on sufferance and for a limited period. On the far right were - and are - the MSI ("Italian Social Movement"), the official heirs to Mussolini's Fascists, but operating within the law and the parliamentary context.

The Italian electoral system was as near to pure proportional representation as any in Europe: a party had only to win a quorum (the overall average of votes per seat) in one constituency for its votes throughout the country to count towards a seat; once over the threshold parties win seats strictly on the basis of votes cast. This system, plus public financing for parties on the basis of votes obtained, encouraged small left-wing parties to remain in the parliamentary game. One, DP (Proletarian Democracy), represented the values of the workers' movements of 1968-9; another, PDUP (Democratic Party of Proletarian Unity), grouping dissidents from the Communist party (from the time of the Hungarian invasion) championed new causes - women's rights, third world issues, ecology) and encouraged the Communist party to take them up.

The same system provided a parliamentary outlet for the Radical Party, which was launched in the 60's as a civil rights movement and "anti-party", not seeking election but using the referendum as a lever for forcing the parties to take up issues they had been afraid to tackle: divorce, abortion and freedom of information in particular. The founder and leader of the Partito Radicale, who ran the party in monarchical style, subservient to his wishes and whims, was Marco Pannella.

The rigidity of the political structure did not mean lack of interest. Italy is the country of the mass membership party. In every district of each city, and even the smallest village, the seat of the local PCI and DC confront each other; and the other parties too will have theirs, where in summer a table and a few chairs stand outside and the party stalwarts come together to talk. Local and national political developments will yield, in an incredibly short time, a blossoming of posters spelling out each party's reactions. The last few years have seen changes in Italian politics to which the image of the breaking log-jam perfectly applies. Particularly unexpected was what happened to the

Italian Communist Party (PCI), starting in the autumn of 1991. The story has echoes in it of the Japanese tradition of ritual suicide. In November 1991 the leader of the PCI, Achille Occhetto, used the wreath-laying ceremony in a village in Tuscany to make a speech in which he said that the Communist Party should change its name, dissolve itself, and link up with other forces in society to form a new party. The method and the content of this pronouncement were both calculated to create a shock-wave that could split the party. Occhetto had consulted none of his senior colleagues in the governing bodies of the party - a breach of the new openness to debate which had marked recent congresses.

As regards the name, if there was one Communist party which did not need to change its name to dissociate itself from the régimes in eastern Europe and the Soviet Union which had begun to crumble, then it was the PCI. The previous summer, it had been the first party to denounce the events on Ti An Min square, and yet had gained votes in the EC elections shortly afterwards. For one member, be he general-secretary, to decree the dissolution of the party, aroused deep feelings on the part of those who had devoted their lives to the political struggle under that banner.The political strategy outlined by Occhetto was equally unwelcome to the more progressive wing of the party. The opening up to new forces and movements - feminists and ecologists in particular - had in fact taken place at the Party's annual congress the previous year. The only serious possibility of new links was with the Craxi's Socialist party, a prospect that was anathema to the left of the party. One third of the membership -a combination of intellectuals and radical young workers engaged in tough shop-floor struggles - came out firmly against Occhetto. With him were most of the party workers, and the old party members from prosperous areas. When the Occhetto line was adopted, many of the opponents felt they must continue the communist tradition, and launched a new party, " rifondazione comunista" (Communist Re-foundation) which attracted the young, radical elements, including many that had stayed aloof from left politics. Rinfondazione was soon winning more than a third of the traditional PCI vote. At the same time, a group of christian-democrat dissidents, known as Rete ("the network") emerged in Sicily and begun to win support.

The fortunes of the PCI were soon overshadowed by the earthquake that shook the Italian political scene. A group of magistrates calling themselves 'mani pulite'(clean hands) began to investigate the extent of bribes("tangenti") in relation to the awarding public works contracts. Soon proceedings had been opened against hundreds of elected politicians Once parliamentary immunity was lifted, many members of parliament finished up on trial or in prison. The peak was reached when former prime minister Andreotti, a symbol of the christian-democrat years, was charged with bribery involving links with the maffia , and socialist leader Craxi was forced to resign. It did not take long for "tangentopoli"' investigations to spread to high officials in the state-owned industries. By then it was clear that, as everyone had known but no-one had dared to say, the christian-democrat state had been corrupt through and through. That was the outcome of decades of uninterrupted rule by the same party. But politicians from all the political parties (with the not quite complete exception of the Communists) had also been involved.

It was also easier against this background to understand the failure of the persistent attempts by the Italian state to master and eradicate the mafia , with its strongholds in Sicily, southern Italy and Naples. Despite some dramatic mass arrests, little progress was made, and the second half of the '80s has seen the mafia extending its activities to the industrialised north of Italy.As the mafia moved north, a new phenomenon has moved south : the "leagues"(leghe) which are movements exploiting the widespread popular dissatisfaction with the traditional parties and with the state. The first of them, the Lega Lombarda, started essentially as a "racist" protest movement against "immigrants" from Sicily and the south taking the jobs of the northerners. But the discriminatory factor has been back-pedalled, and this and other Leagues have concentrated on their critique of the incompetence and corruption of the Italian state. The leagues have made vast political strides, their share of the vote growing from a few per cent to 30% or even 40% in certain areas. By the end of 1992 they were even making inroads into the well-governed and prosperous "red" areas, and threaten to be able to oust the traditional coalition from governing "red" Bologna.

With the parliamentary crisis at its peak, a group of christian-democrats came up with proposals for a total change in the electoral system. Instead of far-reaching proportional representation, Italy would switch to something almost identical with the UK system, of "first past the post", in one-member constituencies, with only one round of voting. Their calculation was that this would ensure the survival of the christian-democrats, who would be the biggest single party in most parts of the country, and the PDS elsewhere. The small parties would be eliminated. In a referendum in the spring, the proposed changes were adopted. But with elections set for March 1994, it was already clear that the c-d's had totally misjudged the situation. For in the meantime, as was revealed by the election of the mayors of the main cities, the political scene had changed beyond recognition. In Rome a MSI (neo-fascist) candidate was beaten by the narrowest of margins by a "green". In Naples it was an ex-Communist (PDS) who just beat Mussolini's grand-daughter, running for the MSI. The line-up for the national elections had the PDS, supported by Rifondazione , the Rete, and the Greens, facing a right that was split between the Lega ,the MSI, and a personal list (populist and anti-communist) headed and financed by the media magnate Berlusconi. Frantic efforts were going on to put together a christian-democrat list with any semblance of credibility.

United Kingdom: farewell to consensus politics

Until recent years, the United Kingdom's electoral system was the object of widespread admiration. The "first-past-the post" voting system with single member constituencies was a guarantee against uncertainty and confusion. Except on rare occasions, it would always yield a workable parliamentary majority on which to base a government. What matter if, because rural constituencies were less populous and urban ones more so, it was possible for a Conservative government to win a majority of seats in Parliament on the basis of a minority of the votes cast ! What matter if a third party - the Liberals, then the Liberal Democrats - could win millions of votes but only a handful of seats. Or that in the elections to the European parliament, using the same system, the Liberals won 11 million votes - and none of the 81 UK seats.

The way in which the two main parties alternated in government, with working majorities, was a guarantee against abuse by parties in power, for whatever they did would become known when the parliamentary majority changed; and this also acted as a check on the powerful centralised civil service.That was to change with the 13 uninterrupted years during which Margaret Thatcher was prime minister. Her approach to politics was a new departure, as was the position from which she operated. British politics had traditionally been based on a consensus about a series of fundamental beliefs and institutions underlying British society: Ms.Thatcher was determined to bring about fundamental changes in the balance of power, and in the beliefs underlying government.Thus one of her avowed aims was to achieve a reduction in the power and influence of the trade unions; another was - in general terms - to dismantle large parts of the welfare state, on the grounds

45

that people should be obliged to look after themselves; third, she was determined to "privatise" a wide range of public services, on the grounds that they would be more efficient and give the public better value for money.

Past prime ministers had been obliged to take account of the balance of power between radicals and conservatives within their own parties: Ms.Thatcher's overall majority in Parliament meant that she could ride roughshod over certain groups within the party, whose views had previously had to be taken into account. In her case it was the "wets" (soft-liners) attached to the idea of a caring state and public services as a state responsibility, whose views could be ignored.

The tough Conservative approach to politics during the Thatcher era resulted in a polarisation which faced the Labour party with a fundamental strategic dilemma. Inevitably, in what is essentially a two-party system, each of the parties is in reality an enforced coalition: better, it has two souls, the reformist and the radical. The reaction of the reformist majority in the ranks of the Labour party was that if the party kept losing elections, it was because it was not offering what the electors wanted. From this it was only a step to suggesting that it was radical attitudes in particular that were at fault. So they must be abandoned. The radical minority, on the other hand, felt that Labour was abandoning its principles. Faced with the injustices and inequalities resulting from Thatcherite rule - the levels of unemployment, the poverty and violence in the inner cities, the running-down of vital social services - Labour should remain true to its principles and offer radical alternatives. The result was a fundamental split in the party. The leadership - especially under Neil Kinnock - rather that trying to build bridges to the radical wing, behaved as though they were afraid to associate with them at all, for fear of Tory propaganda. So the most radical elements, in the "Militant" movement, were expelled from the party, and the leadership made sure that others were not re-chosen as parliamentary candidates. More generally, the fear of radicalism meant that the party was increasingly cutting itself off from the black, feminist, ecologist movements whose natural spokesman it should have been.

With the loss of yet another round of elections, and the immediate choice of a new leader, Labour confirmed that it was going to go on offering a moderate, reasonable image. Under the UK system, this inevitably leaves more radical currents without a political home, and discourages them from all-out commitment to change. On the right, on the other hand, the more extremist right-wing views tend to be accommodated within the party, and to express more or less openly their opposition to the leadership.

The issue of proportional representation flares up periodically in Britain. It was paradoxical that at a time when pressure for "PR" was mounting in the UK, Italy should switch from its proven system of proportional representation should switch to a replica of the UK system, tempered only by the requirement that 25% of the seats be allocated proportionately. Labour seems to find it hard to come to terms with the prospect that under the present system, and with its strategic option to compete for the central political ground, it might well not find itself in government for a very long time.

Netherlands: low profile land

If the criteria for judging whether a country has a democratic system is the existence of parties that adapt to the mood and demands of society, and a lively civil society, then the Netherlands scores high on both counts. The electoral system is proportional, ensuring that small parties can be represented in Parliament. In the '60s and 70's the system was rigid. A party called "Democracy 66" even came into being specifically to channel dissatisfaction with the way the system functioned, often leaving government for many months while negotiations took place in an attempt to put together a coalition with a governing majority. More recently there have been bigger and less predictable swings of opinion.

The party scene is a classic one. A christian-democrat party, which is the biggest, faces a Labour party which has had peaks when it could govern with the support of small left parties, but has gone into decline in recent years and can now expect to be in government only in coalition with the CDs - a return to the post-war situation.

The PR system made it possible for the Netherlands to have a series of small left parties, each winning a few seats in Parliament. One was the new-left PSP (Pacifist Socialist Party), with its origins in the pacifism of the 60s, and a strict socialist ideology. The second, the PPR (Radical party), originated with a small radical splinter group from the Christian-Democrats: its concerns were with the third world, human rights and environmental issues. The third was the CPN (Dutch Communist party), which switched in the 70s from being pro-Moscow to taking an independent "Euro-Communist" line.In the 70s the three parties (plus a small protestant party) began to work together more and more frequently at the level of municipal government. In 1979, they all failed to get seats in the first direct elections to the European Parliament, and this was remedied in 1984 when they ran a single list and

47

won two seats. The successful cooperation between the three at the European level further contributed to the idea of coming together in national politics. Delayed by die-hard resistance in the PSP, the merger was finally achieved in time for the new party to enter the national elections under the name Green Left (Groen Links). Although the total vote initially fell, Green Left has now begun to broaden its support.

The Netherlands has a lively "civil society" and a number of well-established movements around third world, environmental and human rights issues. These movements have in general opted to remain independent of parties, concentrating on mobilising support and seeking to get their concerns accepted by the parties. A measure of the potential of citizen involvement was given by the campaign to "Stop the Neutron Bomb", a cause taken up only in the Netherlands, which succeeded in collecting over a million signatures in a country of 14 million inhabitants. The pressure of movements of all kinds helped to halt the Dutch nuclear programme.

As a founder member of the European Community, the Netherlands has always defended the Community system, which it sees as providing smaller countries with vital procedural guarantees against being ordered around by the big partners. The Dutch were the toughest opponents of De Gaulle's attempts to turn the Community into an inter-governmental organisation. At the same time, they have been the staunchest of "Atlanticists", and uncritical supporters of NATO.

Unravelling Belgium

In the last few decades the Flemish and the Walloons (plus the people of Brussels) have been steadily unravelling Belgium, endowing it with the institutional structures of a federation.This was officially admitted for the first time in the 1993 revision of the constitution, when it was referred to for the first time as a federal state. But in the meantime, over several decades, policy area after policy area has been cut down the middle and handed over to the regional governments. Now, of domestic policies, only social security remains to be regionalised (difficult to solve because not principles but francs are at stake.) That leaves foreign affairs - which for Belgium means essentially their role and interests in the European Community - plus defence.

It took the Belgians a long time to accept that a more federal formula would be preferable to that of the unitary state that had been imposed on them when Belgium became a single country, in 1830. That was after a very brief armed uprising an uprising of its French-speaking population against their Dutch interim ruler. Its powerful neighbours guaranteed its independence in exchange for a commitment to neutrality. But imposing a unitary state on two peoples with different languages and divergent traditions was a recipe for over a century of friction.The recent moves towards a more federal arrangement have been masked by the "very Belgian" expedient of leaving all the institutions of the centralised state, starting with the monarchy, in place alongside the new bodies.For the average citizen the results is a surfeit of democracy, (some might also say a parody of federalism), with elections for local government, for Flemish and Walloon governments, a Belgian national government, and of course for the European Parliament.There also co-exist three regions (Wallonia, Flanders and Brussels) and two communities French-speaking and Flemish-speaking.

All the political parties, previously unified, have split, keeping pace with the federalising trend. The only parties who work together in a single group in the Belgian Parliament are the two ecological parties, Agalev and Ecolo. The dominant force on the political scene have been, and remain, the Flemish christian-democrats (officially "social christians"). They have been able to choose between socialists and liberals (a right-wing variety) to form coalition governments.Their candidate, Wilfried Martens, headed a record of 9 successive governments, before handing over to the previous king-maker, Jean-Luc Dehaene. The socialists have been in government with them periodically, when being away from the spoils of government became to hard to bear. The two socialist parties themselves differ on many issues.In Flanders, a Flemish "nationalist" party, the Volksunie (people's union), played a considerable role in pressing for moves towards federalism. But it had a built-in split between progressive and far-right wings. The Vlaams Blok broke away, and in recent years has taken up racist and extreme right positions. At the national elections in November 1991 it made an unexpected breakthrough, winning 10% overall and 25% in the harbour city of Antwerp, with local peaks of up to 33%. This led to the founding of a citizens' action movement, Charta 91 committed to reviving grass-roots democracy in Flanders.

The Flemish ecological party, Agalev (from the Flemish for "live otherwise"), seems to have hit its ceiling just below 10%: its main preoccupations have been illegal waste dumping and an attempt to win a majority in parliament for an "eco-tax" on packaging, which was headed off by the determined efforts of the industrial lobby. The French-speaking party, Ecolo seemed to find a "natural" level of around 9% of the votes from its very first appearance on the scene, but seldom wins media attention.Since the upsurge of the extreme right in 1991 all three main parties have been seeking an answer to the distrust so clearly expressed by the electors. The result was a shake-up in the political landscape, in which the provisional winner has been the former Liberal party, now calling itself the "citizens' party", while the Volksunie emerged weakened and split. Despite their attempts to renew their image, the governing parties seem not to have been able to restore their fortunes. But nor have the greens managed to turn the situation to their advantage.

Surprisingly, given the presence of the main Community institutions in Brussels, Belgium has not had a high profile in "European" politics. Having been chosen almost by default to host the Council and the Commission, Brussels showed little interest in becoming the real "capital of Europe". This has changed in recent years, above all with the deal under which the European Parliament is being provided with a monster building and all working facilities, while most plenary sessions continue to beheld in Strasbourg, to satisfy the French. There has periodically been talk of a "Washington" type solution, with a "European district". But the other countries will be wary of getting involved in local Belgian politics. As for the Belgians, the kind of gradual, unspoken expansion that has taken place so far is preferable to clear political options and pronouncements.

It might be argued that the Community has paid a high price for this lack of political clarity in terms of uninspired architecture, when building a capital for "Europe", including a building for a parliament, could have been a challenge to the best architects in Europe, or an ideal occasion for a world-wide competition.

4 Families

Thus, for a whole series of reasons, the political life of the European countries has remained isolated, with profound differences of system and of tradition from one country to another. The existential pressures on politicians drive them towards the pinnacles of their national political systems. Language differences help partition the politics of a country from that of its neighbours. What contacts there are tend to be the preserve of "international secretaries" who see themselves as party diplomats, and who monopolise "fraternal" contacts, rather than seeking to create links between members of their parties with the same interests or concerns. At party congresses, where their presence symbolises the shared commitment to international solidarity, the fraternal delegates are more likely to renew their contacts with each other than to meet ordinary delegates from the host country. The network is limited to parties of the same political family; but in any case the contacts remain more formal than operational.

It might have been expected that the drive to unite Europe, and the down-to-earth process of economic integration, would have undermined political barriers, at least between parties in the EC countries. But the impact of unification was not powerful enough to impinge upon national politics or to supplant traditional themes and conflicts. Even the existence of parliamentary bodies at the (western) European level changed little. The Council of Europe has had since 1948 an "assembly" of parliamentarians delegated from national parliaments. The same formula applied until 1979 for the Europan Community. Some of the delegates were convinced "Europeans ; for others the job was a reward for party loyalty or a consolation for not having made it to the top of the political tree. The assemblies carried very little weight.To make the parliamentary assembly of the Community function at all, the traditional political families (socialists, christian-democrats, liberals), which had formed themselves into "political groups," drew on the Community budget to provide those groups with staff and to cover all their operating expenses. But this added to the tendency for them to act in a Euro-vacuum, out of touch with their national parties.

The integration process was marked by the view of Jean Monnet and the other "founding fathers", that to achieve political unity was an over-riding goal, and as such "above politics". Once Europe was united there would be time enough for choosing between policies along party lines: but until then, what mattered was to be for or against "Europe". "Which Europe ? " was a question rarely heard: the very fact of asking it betrayed a departure from the consensus in favour of the predominant liberal society, whose values were inscribed, sometimes explicitly, sometimes by implication, in the Rome Treaty. When the heads of government of the Twelve finally decided to hold direct elections to the European Parliament, starting in 1979, they were seeking to remedy a major fault in the image of the Community system: the absence of legitimate democratic control over the integration process. The elections were an alibi for the power visibly beginning to be wielded by the Council of Ministers and, symbolically at least, by the summit meetings which had begun to be a regular feature of the Community. But it was also a boost to the political groups, not least because it stimulated national political parties to think in terms of fraternal relations with their natural partners from other countries, with whom they would be working together in the European Parliament. Like families making contact with distant relatives, the parties had always linked up essentially according to their family names: socialists, christian-democrats, liberals (the communists were for long refused admission to the club). By the time they became aware that they did not always share the same views or priorities, it was too late for a re-think. Policy disagreements - for instance the split in the socialist family over agricultural policy - have tended to be tactfully avoided, or dealt with in woolly please-all text. Life was harder for the parties which arrived on the European scene without obvious partners - which was the case for those with a strictly nationalist stance - in particular the British Conservatives and the French Gaullists. Nevertheless, the dual incentive to establish a political group - the right to take political initiatives, and access to staff and funding - led to several marriages of convenience. (One of these involved the Irish Fianna Fail party, whose natural place, given its strong Catholic base, would have been in the ranks of the christian-democrats: but that place was taken by the other centre-right Irish party, Fine Gael, and Fianna Fail had no option but to conclude what turned out to be a long-lasting partnership with French

Gaullists.) But in the long run the pressure is for like to link up with like.

The two principal families on the European scene are the socialists (in some countries social-democrats or Labour) and the christian-democrats, formally opponents but often allies in practice, especially within the European Parliament. The number of issues on which there exists a genuine political divide between them has steadily declined.It is within the socialist ranks that deeper confrontations exist, the most marked of all over defence and security. The French socialists have remained staunch supporters of the "force de frappe" (France's nuclear striking force), to which a majority of their colleagues (British, Danish, Greek, some Belgians..) in the socialist group in the European Parliament are opposed, and this has led to clashes within the group and even to contrasting votes in plenary. Over agricultural policy, too, the French, defending the interests of their farmers in the framework of the common agricultural policy, have been at logger-heads with their partners from other groups who have no representatives of farmers interests in their ranks, and blame the Common Agricultural Policy (CAP) for farm surpluses and the soaring EC expenditure on subsidies to farmer. The christian-democrats were for long a more homogenous group, or better able to mask their divergences. The group has a small progressive wing, made up of MEPs with trade union background or support, or from countries like the Netherlands with a greater tradition of social concern. But the majority has not hesitated to cut them down to size, as happened most clearly in the early 80's over Commission proposals for workers' access to information about the plans of multinational companies.

The British Conservatives had always refused to envisage linking up with the christian-democrats - reflecting in this the deep-rooted English Protestant distrust of Catholics and the influence of Rome. But in the context of the European Parliament their group of 30-40 MEPs, plus a couple of makeweights from small conservative parties in other countries (Denmark, Spain..) made them outsiders, wielding little influence. So the "pro-European" majority of the Conservative MEPs were keen to join the ranks of the second-biggest group in the Parliament, with whom in any case they felt ideological affinities. The idea of such a link was favoured by the christian-democrat leaders, and was espoused by UK prime minister John Major at a time where he was trying to establish good relations with Chancellor Helmut Kohl. The outcome, paradoxically, was that the merger finally took place just as Major was adopting his broadly negative stand on the Maastricht Treaty - including the opt-out on the Social Charter - which came under heavy fire from the deeply committed "Europeans" in the christian-democrat group in the Parliament.

Throughout the post-war period the Liberals were seen as the third main political family (the Communists were not counted). Broadly speaking, they have been the party of big capital and big land-owners, their liberalism on economic policy that of the Rome Treaty. Their membership from the Liberal parties in Belgium, the Netherlands or Denmark are far further to the right on economic and social policy than the German or Italian parties, but the group as a whole has a record of commitment about human rights issues. The Liberal group in the Parliament has tended to be dominated, numerically, by the French, since the UDR (Union for the Defence of the Republic), the party of former president Valéry Giscard d'Estaing, found its ideological home there. Only a handful of French MEPs, from the political centre, joined the ranks of the christian-democrats. In 1991 Giscard himself made a surprise move from the Liberals to the Christian-democrats, but only a few of his colleagues followed him. So the French MEPs remain spread over the C-D, Liberal and Gaullist groups. Ideologically, the Gaullists could probably fit in with the christian-democrats, just as the British Conservatives are doing, and the pressure of isolation could move them that way ; but the link-up will only occur if the French right succeeds in presenting a single list in June 1994.

The remaining political family on the right of the political spectrum is the extreme right. Significantly, the group in the European Parliament which brings together (for the moment) only MEPs from Italy, France, Germany and Belgium calls itself the Group of the European Rights - in the plural. It was not long before the attempt to build a group on shared ideas proved a failure, and it opted to be a "technical" group, benefitting from political facilities and practical resources, but not pretending to have a single policy. The only extreme right group to have been present for a long time in the Parliament (even before direct elections) was the Italian neo-Fascist MSI (Social Movement), which as a party with a strong base among Italian migrants to France could not stomach the scarcely veiled racism of Le Pen, and quit the European Right to return to an unattached stance. Several of the Members from the "Republikaner" party in Germany also found Le Pen and his racist stance embarassing when they were trying to rid themselves of a racist label. While there is no doubt that there are many links between neo-Nazi and extreme right groups throughout Europe (and the European Parliament with a series of hearings has helped to make their existence and their activities known), the extreme right parties have not established open links and seem to have difficulties in working together.

On the other side of the political spectrum the place to the left of the socialists is occupied by the Communists. This is another place where there have been major changes in what was previously a rigid pattern. At the time of the first direct elections to the European Parliament, in 1979, there was a single Communist group, the two main components of which were the Italian and French Communists. But "Euro-Communist" Italians and Moscow-oriented French never held joint meetings, had a minimum of contact at the level of staff but not of Members, and put forward different views on most major political issues. The Italians, all from the right of the party (PCI) and under the influence of the old federalist campaigner Altiero Spinelli, were uncritically "pro-European". The French provided a minority voice, strongly critical of Community policies on social and economic issues, relations with the third world and human rights.   The differences became even more marked when in 1992 the Italians insisted on breaking away to form a separate group called GUE (European Unitarian Left), whilst the Group round the PCF opted for title "Coalition of the Lefts" (another plural), or in its English version "Left Unity". Other parties had long since chosen their camp: the Greeks had two Communist parties, roughly matching the two Euro-groups; the Portuguese CP was on the same line as the French; the Spanish Izquierda Unida (United Left), was nearer the Italian line; the Danish Euro-Communist SF (People's Socialist party) had traditional ties with the PCI; and the one representative of the Irish Workers' Party was with the French until after its own split in 1992 when a new member, from Democratic Left, linked up with the GUE.

But the split in the Communist group in the EP was only a mid-way stage. 1990-91 saw the split within the PCI, with the majority following the leadership into a change of name to PDS (Party of the Democratic Left) and an attempt to win acceptance as a potential partner in government. This required joining the Socialist International and.. the Socialist Group in the European Parliament. That left the GUE with the two ex-PCI members who were in the smaller successor party to the PCI, "Rifondazione Comunista", and members from Spain, Greece and Ireland.

The orphaned state of the four parties in the GUE is a reminder of the dilemmas that face the parties whose "family" has genuine policy or ideological affinities, but not even a common name. The designation will vary from country to country -socialist left, new left, or green left. These parties are the inheritors of the ideas of '68 who have also espoused the new causes of the environment, feminism, and non-exploitative policies towards the third world. A small family - its vote in national elections ranging from

3% in the Netherlands to 15% in Denmark - it has a loose but complex European structure. There is one network of "green" parties, and another ('New Left Forum') composed mainly of green left and some ex-Commuist parties. The parties from this family that are represented in the European Parliament have been prevented by national pressures and traditions from forming a single political group. Four, as we have seen, are in the GUE; but the Dutch "Green Left" and the German "Grünen", typical of parties in this family that have a strong eco-socialist commitment, necessarily opt for being in the "Green" group.

The last decade has seen the arrival of "green" parties on the European parliamentary and political scene. Why this has happened, whether it is a sound political option, and whether there is an alternative, are all questions that go to the heart of the issues being raised here about democracy and survival. They go beyond the details of alliances and rivalries in the European Parliament, and merit being dealt with in a chapter apart.

There is one other "family" whose existence is reflected in a political group in the European Parliament - the regionalists, whom it would perhaps be more accurate to refer to as "nationalists". They are the parties whose goal for their region of their nation state and of the Community is one or other formula of national autonomy of independence. Only three of them - Flanders, Scotland and Ireland - were represented in the first directly-elected EP in 1979. To this might be added the Danish "People's Movement Against the European C0ommunity", elected on a platform of Danish withdrawal from the Community to preserve its national autonomy and identity. By 1989 the regionalists had their own political group (taking over the name Rainbow which the Greens discarded), and members representing nationalist/regionalist parties from Corsica, Sardinia and Val d'Aosta, Lombardy, Galicia, the Canary Islands, Euskadi (the Basque country) and Andalucia, and through alliances with them other Spanish regions with autonomous status. Around the group in the European Parliament has been built up a loose organisation, the "European Free Alliance", to develop solidarity among the various parties and movements. But apart from joining forces to make demands relating to the position of the regions in the European Community, there is, almost by definition, little that they can do to help each other, or to acquire a political profile as a single movement.

Thus in the end the political scenery at the European level conforms to the same pattern as at the national level. The myth persists that right and left face each other across a central divide. In reality, faced with the task of running a "free market system" that is proving incapable of achieving its self-appointed goal of continuing economic growth, and incapable too of stemming the structural increase in unemployment, there is little to distinguish the social-democrats from the christian-democrats and their liberal, conservative, Gaullist allies. There is another gulf: on one side of it are the parties that are committed to the free market model, and convinced that the economic crisis will pass and growth return..; on the other are the critics of that system, who realise the inescapable need to change the underlying values and priorities of the economic system, both for reasons of social solidarity and for reasons of sheer planetary survival.

The crucial question then is: what political stance and strategies offer the best chance of introducing those new values and new priorities before it is too late.

For that it is not enough to look at the position of the "green" parties on the political spectrum, and investigate their prospects for achieving fundamental change through democratic institutions. We must also ask whether the option to create "green" parties at all, and play the party political game, was a right one. The move may have been justified tactically for certain movements in certain situations of political immobility.

But that does not mean that it was necessarily right as a strategic choice, when weighed in the light of a series of factors: the levels at which decision-making occurs; the lack of viable international (and/or European) political institutions; and the time-scale on which the struggle against the destructive economic system is being waged. Those who are aware, and care, about the future of the planet and a just and sustainable world society are - potentially - the saving remnant. They, and we, cannot afford to have them make the wrong choice. That is why it seems both necessary and natural to pose those key questions about ecology and politics, and then to explore the significance and potential of the movements within the civil society around these same themes.

5 Greenery

"Green" political parties are only one aspect of a far broader complex of parties, movements, activist groups, and networks, all concerned about the environment - be it local or planetary - which can best be referred to as "green politics". Green politics has been spreading, appropriately, like a fast-growing plant. At the risk of being over optimistic, we could adapt Lester Brown's warning parable about the water lilies.It could well be that awareness and concern about the environmental threat is doubling every day. Certainly it is gaining momentum in a way which is masked by its very diversity. But we do not know how far off is the stage when all humanity will be concerned (albeit out of no higher motive than fear for survival), and whether it will come in time.

The comparis on with the water lily parable is also suspect because the growth there is assumed to be uniform and unstoppable, whereas the spread of environmental awareness and commitment proceeds mostly by unpredictable leaps - more often than not occasioned, it has to be admitted, by the major disasters which force the ecological crisis to the front of the media's priority list, and persuade more people of its gravity. It would probably be more appropriate to liken the progress of environmental awareness to the spread of a rare but resilient species of plant, with seeds that at times fall on fertile soil, take root and flourish, while at others the surroundings are too hostile. It would certainly be over-optimistic to suggest that ecological issues have become central to politics. At best, they have become a source of public awareness and concern, probably replacing fear of nuclear conflict as a lurking source of anxiety. The process that leads from information to awareness, from awareness to concern, and then on to involvement and action, has to happen to individuals, and subsequently to collectivities - local communities, political parties, governments, international

59

organisations. It can give rise to powerful, even potentially irresistible pressure: but the time-scales are disturbingly long. It has taken 25 years and more to reach the present patchy stage - a quarter of a century that is short on the past time-scale of the planet but disturbingly long when we compare it with the accelerating advance of destruction - most of it irremediable - over the same period. There is a frightening gap between awareness and effective action, and it is this that makes it crucial to assess the various approaches that have been tested in practice in Europe over the last 25 years.

There have been three main approaches. One, which could be called the Dutch approach, consists of raising the level of public awareness and commitment about ecological problems, in the hope that public opinion will then force politicians to take the necessary action. The second - the Greenpeace approach - involves a mix of information and direct action about particular issues or situations, putting those responsible (firms or governments) under moral and political pressure to change their ways. The third, associated with the Grünen in Germany, is to enter the political arena directly, on the grounds that traditional parties will not start to act until forced to do so by electoral competition from a growing political movement - one which if successful may even become a decisive partner in government. These approaches are not mutually incompatible, and it is a complex inter-weaving and inter-action of the three that has made ecological issues of all kinds a major source of public concern.

Awareness of the threat to the environment from all kinds of industrial activity probably began in the United States, in the 1960's, with the impact of Rachel Carson's "Silent Spring", and the reputation of Barry Commoner was acquiring as he built up an anti-pollution lobby. Direct protest began, in Europe, in the late 1960's and early '70s, with citizens' action against localised forms of pollution. There were demonstrations about smog in Rotterdam. The villagers of Marckolsheim, on the Alsace side of the Rhine, kept vigil day and night for months in their "round house", built with their own hands on the planned site for a lead plant that had already been chased away from the Netherlands. Not long afterwards the same tactic was used, on the other bank of the Rhine, to block the building of a nuclear power station at Wyhl, on a site in the middle of one of the rare areas of unspoiled woodland in Germany. Local villagers concerned at the impact of cooling towers on their vineyards found themselves allied with anti-nuke militants in defence of their people's house on the projected site.

That was the beginning of the anti-nuke years. Those who took part will never forget the pitched battles around the Brokdorf site near Hamburg, with the organised extreme left leading the ecologists into pitched battles with the police as they tried to drag down the barbed wire barriers round the site. Equally memorable was the dramatic march of sixty thousand demonstrators, in the teeming rain, along the narrow French country lanes leading to Creys-Malville, site of a planned "fast breeder" reactor on the banks of the Rhone north of Lyon. The plant was due to have a core of 5 tonnes of plutonium and the cooling system was to use an equivalent amount of liquid sodium, which catches fire on contact with the air, and is then inextinguishable; and it was less than a hundred km. from Lyon, the second biggest city in France, and from Geneva (but that was across the frontier...). Malville was an international project, with Britain, Italy, and Belgium all holding part of the capital. The demo. too was international, with north German protestors arriving by mini-bus-loads, and hundreds of Italians blocked at the Swiss and French frontiers to prevent their taking part..The confrontation that day was symbolic: on the one side the ultimate in nuclear folly, on the other the biggest ecological demonstration France was to have. As the marchers neared the site, they began to hear the thuds of exploding percussion grenades, and from time to time an ambulance sped down the lanes, scattering the marchers into the muddy fields. The French riot police had chosen their site in the best Napoleonic tradition, holding a bridge over a stream. Small groups of demonstrators, equipped for combat, armed with stout staves and with face-masks dipped in lemon juice against the tear-gas, clashed with the police in a meadow, whilst tens of thousands who had come for a non-violent demonstration looked on from the slopes. Then the police began to charge, firing explosive grenades into the ranks of the watchers, and then driving them back in panic through the maize-fields. A young Frenchman was killed outright by a grenade that collapsed his lungs, and another had to have his foot amputated.The message from the French state was clear: "Hands off Malville", which was central to the plans of the nuclear lobby - and formed an important link in the French atomic weapon strategy. For the anti-nuke movement the march on Malville was traumatic: as though in tacit recognition that you could not take on the might of the state, there would not be another big anti-nuke demo.in France. As for the fast breeder, it has been plagued by accidents and hardly ever functioned.Over the years there came too the series of accidents: the near melt-down at the Three Mile Island nuclear reactor, and the near-miss (largely hushed up) of a nuclear conflagration at the La Hague re-processing plant in Normandy; the release of poisonous chemicals at Bophal in India, at Seveso in Italy, at the Sandoz plant on the Rhine in Switzerland; the giant oil tanker shipwrecks from the

Torrey Canyon to the Amoco Cadiz. All of these helped to bring the risk of large-scale accidents home to a wider public, but a more fundamental realisation, of the destructiveness of our industrial system when it is functioning "normally", has yet to come. Pollution of the seas was probably the first of these general problems to be identified, as early as the 70s, but the threat was too remote, and awareness only came with the dramatic super-tanker spills, even though in quantitative terms the unending flow of oil and other pollutants into the seas, and its destructive impact on marine food-chains, is far more serious. The most recent phase has been the breakthrough at all levels -person-in-the-street as well as politicians- to an awareness of problems which endanger the whole planetary ecosphere. Increasing numbers of people know and are concerned about the destruction of the rain forests - "the lungs of the earth": among the TV sequences that have caught the imagination is the satellite film of the pall of smoke from 7000 simultaneous fires burning as the settlers eat their way into the Amazon forests. The most recent, and the most widely known, are the "green-house effect", with its threat of rising water-levels; and the damage to the ozone layer, which if it proves to be increasing will constitute a direct personal threat that is likely to bring greater involvement than the rise of sea-levels at some relatively distant date.The stages of awareness did not succeed each other but overlapped and inter-twined, and awareness did not spread at the same rate, or with the same priorities, throughout Europe. In general, the northern countries had a big lead over the south in terms both of the level of information about ecological issues and of public involvement. But the stage that has occurred, sooner or later throughout Europe, has been the launching of "green" political parties, with their particular impact on the political landscape and the attitudes of the main parties, their electoral successes - and their dilemmas.

Enough experience has been acquired, by now, to permit an assessment of the various approaches to bringing ecological issues onto the political scene. The three approaches already mentioned have in fact been practised in the very different contexts of the different countries, and with varying success. The first option was that taken by the environmentalists in northern European countries - in particular Denmark, the Netherlands, and the United Kingdom. These were the countries where well-organised, powerful movements have traditionally grown up around specific issues - and have chosen to concentrate on informing and mobilising public opinion, leaving it to the political parties to take the issues on board and work them into their political platforms. Exemplary of this trend was the OOA (Organisation for information on Nuclear Energy) launched in Denmark in the 1970's to oppose plans for nuclear power stations in Denmark. After over a decade of campaigning it was successful, despite the initial pro-nuclear stance of virtually all political parties, including the powerful social-democrats. Part of the explanation lies in a stroke of luck - or genius: the "Smiling Sun" symbol. The yellow badge, with its simple smiling face and the slogan "Atomic Power - No thanks", was sold to finance a campaign in Denmark. (Later it was to spread all over the world, and a small slice of the proceeds helped launch an international news network against nukes and in support of alternative energy strategies - WISE, the World Information Service on Energy - which still functions).From the start, OOA's target was to get its message to all Danes, and in the closing stages of its campaign it did actually make a mailing of an impressive multi-chrome folder, with the arguments against nuclear power, to every household in the country. The party bosses and the technocrats were reluctant to give up the coveted membership of the European nuclear energy "club", but OOA's campaign had turned the referendum, which they had been counting on, into a double-edged weapon they could not risk using. There was also growing mobilisation against the Danish project in the densely-populated southern tip of Sweden. So the plans for Denmark's first nuclear power station were finally dropped. More generally, environmental issues were taken up, not by all parties in the political spectrum, but essentially by the People's Socialist Party, which was more open to contact and information from those concerned particularly with the environment.

The Netherlands has always had a proliferation of lively one-issue movements. It also has a level of concern about people's physical surroundings which springs from the fact that land reclaimed from the sea, but situated below sea-level, is a precious asset. It was not long before the many local initiatives around environmental issues began linking up, and one result was an influential umbrella organisation called "Milieu Defensie" (Defence of the Environment) with its own monthly magazine. At the height of the struggle about nuclear energy - when the immediate goal was to prevent a new plant from being started up - there were a series of specifically anti-nuke organisations, including "Women against nuclear power" and even "Old Age Pensioners against nukes". In the Netherlands, as in Denmark, although there is a greater readiness to welcome ecological issues than there is in most other parts of Europe, it is again the smaller left-wing parties (in the Dutch case the three that were to merge to form the "Green Left") that have really made the issues their own.

Into party politics

The story of the Grünen (the German greens) is central to this discussion, for it illustrates many of the arguments for and against the green movement moving into electoral politics. The decision to go political arose initially from a strange alliance. On one side were a mass of local environmental groups, in the "friends of nature" tradition, recruiting their membership from solid usually bourgeois citizens. Their umbrella organisation, the BBU ("Bundesverband der Burgerlichen Umweltausschussen" or Federal organisation of citizens' environment committees), soon found itself involved in the struggle against nuclear power plants and there began to be talk of founding a party. On the other side were a range of left-wing political groups, which had effectively led the resistance to nuclear installations. In northern Germany in particular, a range of "post-'68" groups - ecologists, feminists, gays and lesbians, peace movement activists, alternative schools - had begun to link up to contest local elections. They had a shared experience of the unreceptiveness not just of the state apparatus but also of the political parties, including the social-democrats (SPD). When the Young Socialists (JuSo's) began to take up these themes of new politics, there was a clamp-down by the party. It was this blockage that made all these various strains share the conclusion of former student leader Rudi Dutschke, that the alternative movements had to opt for "the long march through the institutions." So when the decision to found a party was finally taken, in the mid-70s, it was a coalition of a wide range of movements, and of individual arriving from other parties such as the Young Socialists. The German language has a useful word, bunt, meaning "multi-coloured", and the groups linking forces in northern Germany had stood as Bunte Listen (multi-coloured lists). But the ecological stream feeding into the new party needed to mark itself off from the left, and those who came from the ideological left knew they must keep a low profile - whence the option to call it Die Grünen. This was to be the source of a major misunderstanding. When the Grünen, to the astonishment of the political class, leaped the 5% hurdle to sweep into the Bundestag (the Federal Parliament) in 1978 with 29 members, it gave an enormous boost to environmental movements throughout Europe. But it was widely assumed that the Grünen, as their name implied, were essentially a "green" or environmentalist party, rather than (as they were in fact) an alternative left party, one important strand of whose platform was concern for the environment. So in countries where there was no similar "multi-coloured" potential, the success of the German "greens" encouraged the founding of what those more to the left within the Grünen called "bottle-green" or "green green" parties, claiming to be "above" the traditional right-left political divide, and even hostile to the left.

The early years of the Grünen were marked by fierce in-fighting, which they did not even try to hide from the public, between two opposing tendencies known as Fundi's (fundamentalists) and Realo's (realists): The former saw is as a betrayal to go into coalition with other parties: the role of the Greens should be to criticise from outside, and go on building up their support until they could govern. The latter were convinced that where Greens could influence events by joining a coalition or giving their parliamentary support (on terms), then they should do so. It is in the Netherlands that things seem to have worked out best. In 1984, when the three small Dutch left parties (Pacifist Socialists, Radicals and Communists) were running a joint list for the elections to the European Parliament, there was an attempt to launch a Dutch green party. But there was no real hope of supplanting the three, all of which had taken up environmental issues. When the formal merger of the parties finally took place, the new party opted to call itself the "Green Left" (Groen Links). Things might have been clearer if the Germans when founding their party had made the same choice.

The story of the French "greens" could hardly have been more different from that of the Germans. With one or two striking exceptions (the struggle for survival of the Larzac sheep-farmers, or the march on the Malville fast-reactor site), there was little ecological activity in France at any level in the '70s or even the '80s. At the European Parliament elections of 1979, when facing hurdles that were both financial (requirement to pay their own voting forms and basic leaflet) and political (5% minimum to win seats at all) the green vote was under 4% French intellectuals, too, were many years behind in becoming aware of planetary ecological issues, which suddenly emerged as politically fashionable at the start of the '90s. There has been no question in France of a broad-based and effective ecological movement opting to go into electoral politics. From the start, the French "greens" thought in terms of a political party. After several attempts with parties that folded, they finally got their act together as a party, and opted to carve themselves a piece of the traditional political scene. They started with a few successes in municipal elections, then at regional level. But they were deeply divided. On the one side were those who saw the traditional parties as being equally responsible for the fate of the environment, and an ecological party as marking itself out from traditional politics. On the other were those who saw themselves as being of the left. Rather like the German party, they were rift by deep divergences over their strategic stance.There were: should they continue to proclaim " a-plague-on-both-your-houses", or be prepared to make compromises. In France, with the two rounds system, the option arises at the second round, if there is a left versus right run-off: the green party has to decide whether to call on its voters to switch to the socialist, leave the choice free, or recommend abstention.

In the 1991 regional elections, the Greens were actually in a position to conclude a coalition with the socialists in several regional assemblies, and one green candidate, in the north, became president of the regional assembly on the basis of an alliance with the Socialists. The campaign for those regional elections saw a development for which there had been no precedents elsewhere: the emergence of two ecological parties, running neck-and-neck, and poaching votes from all the traditional parties. One was "les Verts " (the Greens), led by Antoine Waechter, definitely a "green green" with no sympathy for the left, who had been their candidate in the previous round of presidential elections. The other was a movement called "Génération Ecologie", put together by Brice Lalonde, the first ecologist to become widely known, one-time presidential candidate, who had been brought into the Rocard government. His decision to put together a party of his own was tactical and well-timed, coming when the socialists were going into steep decline. Those on his list were mainly well-known local or national personalities, many of them new to politics - another "party of notables". With the two parties together winning a totally unexpected share of the votes, and the polls showing the socialists likely to sink to around 20%, there was every incentive for the two green parties to link up, and after negotiations between Waechter and Lalonde (not the first sin of centralism they would commit), an agreement was reached on joint candidates in almost all constituencies. In the meantime the effective leadership of the Greens had moved from Waechter to Dominique Voynet, a potential presidential candidate, who made it seem a natural choice to support the socialists - not least because in that way they could help limit the inevitable landslide victory of the right.This proved to be an illusion, and early in 1994, with the European elections looming, the "Verts" were more divided than ever.

In Italy, awareness of ecological issues occurred later than in northern Europe, having, as we shall see, no tradition of civil involvement outside the sphere of the political parties. The situation was soon confused, with the "green" members of parliament asserting their autonomy, and two separate and competing green movements.All the existing left or alternative movements, including Communists, Radicals and Democrazia Proletaria, sought to attract the green vote. The result has been that no single credible green party has emerged.

Things were not dissimilar in Spain, where active ecological groups are scarce, and would-be political parties are numerous, none of them able to win a significant proportion of the vote, but all of them incapable of coming to terms to build a single party; meanwhile, the United Left has integrated ecological concerns well enough to be attracting the green vote.

In the end it is difficult to draw hard and fast conclusions about the various possible green strategies. There have certainly been situations where opting to go into parliamentary politics seemed justified. Essentially, this was when society in general, and the traditional parties in particular, were refusing to respond to the pressure of growing numbers of concerned citizens. On the face of it, this was what happened in the German Federal Republic: but the option was probably inherent in a pact in which one of the components was people from radical left backgrounds who necessarily thought in terms of a strategy for advancing their ideas in the framework of the democratic political system.Another aspect of the German experience that merits reflection concerns the practical impact of success. In the '60s and early '70s it had been the Young Socialists (in the SPD) who had elaborated a dual strategy: direct action, around locally sensitive issues, as a complement to the traditional political game. In their case, it had run into inflexibility of the party and of social structures. What happened with the Grünen was different. Several things combined to catapult them into the role of a major national party. One was the size of their "natural" constituency -a wide range of ecologists and a wide range of disillusioned people from the left - which meant that they started off with 27 members of parliament. Another was the generous financing (on the basis of votes won) and practical facilities (such as staffing) with which the German system rewards those who leap the 5% hurdle. This plethora of resources was also a trap. Apart from the 27 Members, and their 27 "alternates" (who the Greens wanted to take over, on the principle of "rotation", half-way through the legislature), they had to recruit 27 parliamentary assistants, and fill all the posts to which they were entitled: suddenly, they had a staff of over 100. The result was a "vacuum-clearer effect" as committed and dynamic party members and supporters from all over the country were sucked into the brand new party machine in Bonn. The grass-roots aspects of the Greens' activity was virtually decapitated, with an effect like a political purge in reverse. Coping with their responsibilities in the parliamentary system was hard to reconcile with a continued commitment to direct action on local issues, and there was not a second wave of activists to step into their shoes. The next few years, when the Grünen were making their mark in the parliament, breaking taboos and bringing a breath of procedural and vestimentary fresh air, there was a sudden drop of the level of activity on environmental issues.

Did the Grünen then have a bigger impact by going into traditional politics than they would have done if the same amount of talent and commitment had continued to go into struggles around a wide range of environmental, social and human rights issues ? On the one hand, pressure from the presence of the Greens in parliament seems not to have obliged the other parties - even the social-democrats, to take up "green". (The fact that Germany has backed off from nuclear power is almost certainly due above all to rising costs - occasioned mainly, it is true, by the delays imposed by the legal rearguard battles of local citizen action groups).

In northern Europe, the evidence is that the option for environmental and other campaigners to remain "one issue movements", persuading and winning support right across the spectrum of society, and thus weighing on the parties to espouse their cause, has turned out to be the right one. Conversely, in southern European countries with little tradition of citizen involvement, there is a strong case for saying that what is needed is more local groups fighting on specific issues, rather than more people playing at politics in a mass of small parties which offer no real prospect of influencing what happens.

Suggestions for a strategic option around this issue, will have to form part of a broader estimation of the role and impact of civil society (and not just environmental movements) in relation to the political future of Europe.

6 Civil society

Dedicated bird-watchers holed up in the marshes, protecting the first few nests of a warbler that has returned to its former haunts..; women camped in the dead of winter along the perimeter of a US Air Force site in Britain, waiting to block the arrival of nuclear missiles; 'beurs' , second generation immigrants, marching from Marseilles to Paris to assert their rights as French citizens; activists using limpet mines to sink illegal Spanish whaling vessels; three thousand environmental campaigners from the world over, converging on the "earth summit" in Rio to demand radical measures to save the planet..

The term "civil society", originally coined by Italian marxist theorist Antonio Gramsci, has come into broader use in recent years because it reflects a vital reality. Groups of citizens are determined to exercise their influence on events, acting together outside the "official" framework of the state and its institutions, including the political parties. The range and liveliness of its "civil society" is a measure of the vitality of a country's democracy. The civil society has asserted itself in the European dimension without waiting for the founding of a state, and has come to grips with the existing but inadequate institutional machinery.

There is an infinite range of groupings and activities that fall under the broad description of "civil society"; and the range varies greatly from one part of Europe to another. The United Kingdom and the Netherlands have by far the richest traditions, followed by the Nordic countries. In France, on the other hand, the kind of problems which in Britain or Denmark might result in the creation of an association of concerned citizens would tend to be left to the all-knowing and all-providing state, as personified by the préfet for the area. At best, there will be corporatist organisations, like those defending the interests of the hunters. In southern Europe it is often the political parties, with their strong local presence, that take up issues and create organisations. The extreme example of this is "ARCI" the Italian Association for Recreation and Culture - set up and guided jointly by the Communist and Socialist parties. It currently has over a million members, and is responsible for a wide range of citizen activities.

A striking exception to the rule that France has little in the way of civil society was provided during the '70s when a group of French sheep farmers, in a decade-long struggle, successfully resisted being driven out to make way for the extension of a military training camp.It was a copy-book struggle, illustrating all the creative potential, but also the pitfalls to be avoided, in a clash between a group of citizens defending their livelihood and a remote and arrogant central authority, prepared to treat parts of its country as it had done its colonies.

The army already occupied a large part of the sparsely inhabited Larzac plateau. In 1970 plans were announced for an extension of the camp, requiring the expropriation of 102 shepherds, who made their living by supplying milk to a plant down in the valley producing the green-veined Roquefort sheep's cheese. Most of the shepherds had been there for generations, and there was a leaven of new arrivals who had chosen to leave the city for the simplicity of life on the plateau, with the big herds of tough, scraggy, upland sheep - a far cry from their barrel-shaped lowland cousins of the Kent marshes or the dykes of northern Holland.

A solemn declaration from the 102, that they would not leave their land, marked the start of a triple learning process - for the shepherds, for those who supported them, and for the French military and civil authorities. Very early on, the "102" understood that although support was welcome and necessary, they had to retain control over their own struggle.They discovered the force of political symbolism : how a ring of fires on the cliffs round the local town of Millau would awake the citizens to what was going on upon the plateau; or how a march to Paris and a flock of Larzac sheep grazing beneath the Eiffel Tower could mean the breakthrough to national media attention. They incorporated into their approach the non-violence preached by the larger-than-life figure Vasco de Gama, lifelong crusader for non-violence. Realising the links between their struggle to retain their land and the problems of hunger in the world, they ploughed up and sowed neglected fields belonging to the army or to absentee land-owners, and sent the crops to third world countries. They also established links of solidarity with the independence movements in New Caledonia, far away in the Pacific - one of those colonised corners of the world still formally part of France

The dispute over the Larzac site was soon known all over France. Efforts by political parties to take over the cause were given short shrift. Instead, independent Larzac support committees sprang into existence in towns and cities throughout France and beyond, with most of their membership composed of people not affiliated to any political party. Every summer the supporters gathered in their thousands at a natural amphitheatre on the plateau for debates and social activities. Many people took shares in organisations which bought up land on the plateau and helped instal young shepherds, who benefitted from a French government support scheme. At the heart of the Larzac, volunteers helped to provide one of the farms with a sheep stall of grandiose proportions, looking more like a chapel. For creating a sense of solidarity, there was nothing to match having mixed cement and helped lay the solid walls of local stone. The struggle lasted for a decade, with continual skirmishes, but the solidarity of the shepherds was never really shaken. In the end, it was the French President, François Mitterrand, who over-rode the objections of his military advisers and formally buried the extension plan

Marching against the missiles

Different in the extreme, as an expression of the civil society, was the protest movement against plans for the stationing of Pershing 2 and Cruise missiles in western Europe, as a response to presence of Soviet missiles in the Comecon countries. Within the space of a few months, in 1981, millions of European citizens - many of whom had never taken part in marches or demonstrations - had taken to the streets to make their opposition known to governments and parties.There was a complex background to this NATO initiative and the resistance which it sparked off. There had been signs of restiveness among the United States' allies in NATO. When the Americans decided on deploying the new missiles, they adopted for land sites, rather than deploying them at sea, which was a viable alternative. They chose sites in the countries where the governments were the most amenable (the Federal Republic, the United Kingdom, Italy and Belgium). The message was clear: Uncle Sam still called the tune.

But the American and NATO authorities misjudged the mood of European opinion. Ordinary citizens had understood one simple fact: that Europe ran the risk of becoming the battle-field for a nuclear conflict between the super-powers. In almost all western European countries there was a generation that

71

had come of age politically demonstrating against the Vietnam War, and the networks and traditions were still intact. Even so, no-one could have predicted the scale of the wave of protest, with over a million marching in Bonn and in Rome, many hundreds of thousands in Amsterdam and Brussels, and hundreds of thousands more in unreported marches in smaller towns and cities all over western Europe. In Brussels, nuns in their habits followed hard-line Mao-ist groups, and coach-loads of Kurdish migrant workers from Koln waited patiently for hours to bring up the rear of the procession. Over the same period, the sites which had been chosen for installing the Pershing 2 and Cruise missiles became focal points for opposition. The most colourful was Greenham Common, in the UK, where women from the peace movement set up a camp besieging the site, continually provoking the military, and refusing to be driven away. A network of links with people in surrounding towns and villages meant that material to equip the site could not be moved around without being blockaded. The Greenham Common experience, and that at other less well-known sites had a major impact in informing the public about what was at stake, and mobilising against the missiles.

Camps and direct action are hardly a part of the political traditions of Sicily, particularly not those of the Communist party, who were in power at Comiso, the town near which Italy's share of the contested missiles were to be installed. But under pressure from peace movement activists, even the Communist councillors found themselves gathering to protest, and being violently dispersed by the police.

Out of the demo's of 1981 and 1982 grew another initiative that has a lot to show about the potential of civil society movements for working together across frontiers. Although there was minimal liaison to ensure that the big demo's did not clash, there was no machinery for on-going contact between those who took part in the demo's, or even between those who were responsible for organising them. Luciana Castellina, a dissident from the Italian Communist party, and member of the European Parliament, and Ken Coates, founder of the Institute for Workers' Control and of the Bertrand Russell Peace Institute, set out to remedy this situation. They contacted all those who had signed the "Bertrand Russell Appeal" (written by Coates, historian Edward Thompson, and academic Mary Kaldor) calling for a Europe free of nuclear weapons, from the Atlantic to the Urals. The aim was to call hold a large-scale meeting of people who had been involved in the marches and demo's - a European Convention on Nuclear Disarmament. The practical organising was entrusted to agenor, a multi-nationality group which had acquired expertise in organising multi-lingual meetings of people from

72

different backgrounds. An International Liaison Committee was established to plan and supervise the preparations.

The first Convention, attended by over a thousand people from all over Europe, was held in Brussels. In the years that followed, Conventions were held annually: in Berlin, Perugia, Amsterdam, Coventry, Paris, Lund, Vitoria-Gasteiz (in the Basque country), Helsinki-Tallinn, and Moscow. The Liaison Committee developed into a body unique in Europe, where representatives of peace movements, political parties (social-democrats, communists, greens), church organisations, and trades unions - many of whom could not previously have envisaged sitting down together - met every two months to thrash out the programme of the next Convention. With membership ranging from the PCI (Italian Communist party) to the Dutch (Protestant) Inter-Church Peace Council, voting was out of the question. As the participants came to know more of the context in other countries, it became easier to work together, and to work by consensus. For nearly a decade there was a built-in tension in the Liaison Committee and the Conventions between movements who had close contacts with independent civil rights groups in eastern European countries, and those (social-democrats in particular) who wanted to involve the official peace movements, linked to the Moscow dominated World Peace Council. In the end the barriers fell, and at the end of the 80's, Liaison Committee meetings and the Conventions became a place where "officials" and "independents" could sit at the same table.

Historians of the peace movement have concluded that the vast spontaneous manifestation of public concern, at the start of the 80's, made a direct contribution to the ending of the Cold War and the Soviet initiatives leading to disarmament. The scale of the demo.s, and the strength of the ground swell of opinion which they reflected, revealed a growing dissatisfaction in western countries with the aggressive stance of the Reagan administration. Michael Gorbachov, for his part, seized the importance of the peace movement, studied its development and took over many of its ideas in working out his case for disarmament. The peace movements were of course aware that success could be fatal to them. Once the immediate threat of nuclear conflict on their soil had been removed, the vast majority of those who had marched in the demo.s were happy to return to their role of informed but essentially passive citizens, and were prepare to leave responsibility for further rounds of disarmament with the governments. The Liaison Committee saw a steady decline in the number and importance of the organisations represented at its meetings; but the hard core which remained broadened the scope of its concerns. The annual Conventions continued, tackling such issues as the role of the United Nations in promoting world peace; the links between arms trade, security, and third world development; and problems of nationalism and racism. The Conventions also became an invaluable forum for nascent civil rights and environmental groups in central and eastern Europe and the former Soviet Union to meet their potential partners from the west.

United against racism

Among the most significant expressions of popular concern has been the varied and widespread reactions against the upsurge of racism. In France, faced with a wave of shootings of immigrants by trigger-happy cops or gun-toting citizens acting in "legitimate self-defence", the reaction took the form of a mass movement of second generation migrants, known as "SOS Racisme". Addressing itself to all "beurs " - Arab, black of white -it rapidly became of country-wide organisation, and its founder and leader, Harlem Désir, a nationally known figure. The movement undoubtedly succeeded in its aims of giving the beurs a sense of identity, and getting across to opinion their wish to be treated like other French citizens. Later, with "SOS Racisme" under fire for being too dependent on support from the Socialist party, other groups emerged. In Italy, where the new wave of racism took the form of attacks on illegal African immigrants, it is ARCI , the communist/socialist organisation promoting popular culture, that has been foremost in organising mass demonstrations to denounce racism. In Germany, the country-wide outbreak of attacks on immigrant families was met by an impressive series of spontaneously organised marches and candle-light vigils, involving not just young people but a cross section of the adult population, exerting moral pressure on the politicians to ensure a tougher police reaction. A reaction essentially confined to Britain was the anti-racist commitment of popular groups and musicians, developing into a nation wide "Rock Against Racism" concert. Mammoth concerts, televised round the world, have been one of the most interesting and effective expressions of civil society. They began with Bob Geldorf's "Band Aid" concert, to raise funds to fight famine and deprivation in the third world - an operation which mobilised an impressive list of international stars, and enabled people to have a direct impact in disaster areas. A concert held to welcome the South African opposition leader Nelson Mandela when he was released after 25 years in prison, took the potential of the formula a step further: transmitted world-wide, it gave Mandela the biggest audience ever for a political speech, in which he called for the support of the world community. This was certainly one of the first manifestations of a potential world-level civil society.

There is little doubt that civil society organisations of every kind flourish in times of prosperity, when people feel sure of themselves and are not subject to the economic squeeze of a recession. Because they largely depend on individual payments, either once-off gifts or membership dues, their resources decline as unemployment spreads. They also rely to a large extent on dedicated, unpaid, volunteer work, and this dwindles as the economic situation worsen. It is striking that despite the unprecedented levels of unemployment, and the mounting wave of sackings, there has been a relative lack of imaginative reaction by the workers. Most trade unions, in their attitudes, have an "establishment" rather than a civil society mentality. Where there has been resistance it has come directly from the workers. More interesting, in the British miners' strikes, first in the '70's, then again in 1982-3, against threatened pit closures, resistance was stiffened by women's support committees, not only organising practical support on the spot, but boosting the strikers' morale, and getting their message to a wider audience.

This chapter did not set out to chronicle the full range and scope of civil society. It recalls a few of the more original or spectacular events and movements that have had a real impact on a particular situation, by acting outside the framework of official structures, and developing new forms of self-organised response.

7 Myths and policies

Whatever new political unit emerges in Europe in the coming years, it is going to be built on the existing European Community. What happened in the negotiations on the Maastricht Treaty is a striking pointer to the future. A majority of the member states (effectively all but the Netherlands and Belgium) ostensibly sought to make of the European Union a new, parallel, inter-governmental structure. But when it came to the crunch there turned out to be a far-reaching consensus on not complicating matters by creating a whole new complex of institutions. So the European Union is based on the institutions of the Community. The passing decades, with their myriads of meetings of experts, civil servants and ministers, have made of the Community a decision-making machine which, cumbersome though it is, does work. To have tried to create a new, parallel intergovernmental structure would have resulted in chaos. So the Commission will not only continue to play its central role in the workings of the Community: it can be expected to play a similar role in the Union. Of a leap to a genuinely federal structure, with a Commission voted in by a majority in the Parliament, there was no question: the idea was not even on the agenda.

Likewise, the policies that come out of Brussels will be influenced as in the past by conflicting pressure groups, and will reflect the balance of national interests, as it emerges from the horse-dealing around the Council table. Predictions about how the Community will develop, or alternative proposals for how it ought to develop, need to be grounded in a critical understanding of how and why key Community policies turned out as they did.

The Community started at the end of the '50's with a Treaty remit that covered only a limited number of policies: removal of barriers to trade within the area, and freeing of trade at the world level; enforcement of free competition throughout the EC area; regulation of trade in agricultural produce and concern for the farming community and for food supplies; coordination of monetary policy ; and modest pretensions about limiting the negative impact of freer trade in terms of regional disparities and social problems. Since then its mandate has taken on broader dimensions, sometimes at the Commission's initiative, sometimes at the instigation of the member States, sometimes again as a reaction to proposals from the European Parliament. The removal of trade barriers alone has given way to the more ambitious target of eliminating all obstacles to the movement of persons, services, and capital within the Community area. Coordination of economic policy has been extended to cover the far more arduous task of bringing about a convergence of member States' economic policies. Social and regional policies now involve spending on a far wider scale. Environmental policy - or at least certain aspects of it - has belatedly acquired far greater importance, with scope for majority voting. The Community has begun to weave a network of special relations, usually involving some trade concessions and some financial support, with countries in all parts of the world facing economic difficulties - not least of course the fragments of the former communist empire.

To judge from the past four decades, there are as many patterns of negotiations and influence as there are policy areas. It is traditional for the "Europeans" to regard a policy which has been worked out and applied at the Community level as the optimum ,or at least preferable (though they have now to come to terms with the commitment to the "subsidiarity" principle - all decisions to be taken as near the citizen as possible.) The Common Agricultural Policy was for long presented as a model, because decision-making had been transferred from the national to the European level. This sort of praise only came to be played down as the costs of the policy got out of hand.

What has been missing is a critique of the various policies, not in terms of how "European" they were, but according to the extent to which they were shaped by pressure groups and national interests.

But before venturing into an examination of Community policy-making in key sectors a reminder of the nature of the Community institutions and the relations between them is probably not superfluous.It is important to break with the clichés about all-powerful bureaucrats in Brussels usurping the democratic rights of national parliaments. The Community is a peculiar construction, based on a partial transfer of sovereignty, and it has to be recognised as such. But one of the difficulties for the lay person (however concerned with things "European"), and one of the reasons for the remoteness of the Community, lies in the fact that the relationship between the institutions does not correspond to any pattern familiar to the citizens of the "12" -nor indeed of tomorrow's "16" or more.

An institutional no-man's land

The leading roles are played by the European Commission, the European Parliament, the Council of Ministers and - where major options are at stake - the "European Council" of the heads of government (with the French President). Supporting roles are played by the Court of Justice and the Court of Auditors (formally designated "organs of the Community"). There is also a European Economic and Social Committee, comprising representatives of trade unions, employers and "other interests" such as farming, but carrying little weight; and the Maastricht Treaty brought into being a "Committee of the Regions" with a similar subordinate status, which seems destined from the start to be equally marginal
  While the constitutional pattern in parliamentary democracies varies according to the origins and past history of each state, most have in common:

- a democratically elected parliament;
- an executive (government), which is either directly elected (US) or reflects the political majority in the parliament,as it results from elections.
- in some cases a second chamber - intended to exercise a moderating role or reflect regional interests.

  If we go looking for parallels it is necessary to tread cautiously. The Commission is not, as it might seem, the executive (or embryonic government) of the Community, though it has, under different presidents, aspired more or less openly to such a role. It's main formal task is to take the initiative in making proposals for Community legislation, and to follow its proposals through the decision-making machinery that involves the Council and the Parliament. In certain areas (trade policy in particular, bilateral agreements with third countries, and participation in international bodies), it does represent the Community. There are also narrowly defined areas of domestic policy where it has an executive function - bits of farm policy in particular. It has, too, to play a "watch-dog" role, to see that member states observe and carry out Community legislation - and if not to take them before

79

the Court of Justice. Not least, in recent years it has come to be accepted (in the person of its president) as an equal partner in the regular "summits" of the Twelve. This was a predictable trend, since the Commission is in the best position to speak for the Community as a whole, but it also owed a lot to the standing and the solidity of Jacques Delors as President.

It is equally difficult to find a parallel for the Council of Ministers. It shares with the Parliament the task of adopting (or amending, or refusing) the proposals tabled by the Commission. It is certainly not an embryonic government. It is more like an arena where ministers defend their national interests (with the Commission as honest broker to defend the interests of the Communist as a whole.There is not one Council of Ministers, but one for each policy area. The Council could well, in the future, become a second chamber, sharing the legislative role with the Parliament. Over the years there has been a gradual shift to majority voting in the Council on key policy areas (environment, social affairs, internal market..). But the complex system of weighted voting provides effective guarantees that countries in a minority will not be steam-rollered by the majority - or the smaller countries bullied by the larger ones.

The status of the Parliament is perhaps the most misleading of all. The very essence of a parliamentary system is that the government derives its legitimacy from an electoral majority, resulting from elections. This is not the case in the Community. As the system currently works, there has been no link between the results of the elections to the European Parliament (which has a five-year time of office), and the mandate of the Commission (appointed for four years by .. the member States). Parties have not been able to present credible alternative programmes, because the elections leave the composition and policies of the Commission unchanged. In 1994, for the first time since direct elections to the European Parliament began in 1979, the mandates of the Commission and the Parliament will coincide. The candidate for President of the Commission agreed upon by the governments will then be endorsed by the Parliament. What this means is that the member States have baulked at letting the Parliament designate the President and his/her team - the only way of giving them democratic legitimacy, and letting the voters choose between different programmes.

Like so much in the Community, the Commission exists in a sort of institutional no-man's-land. It is a creature of the governments, which appoint it, but its total independence is underlined by an oath before the Court of Justice. The President is chosen by the governments, and the Commission is supposed to practice collective responsibility. But the President has little say over the nominations made by the governments for the other 16 posts. She/he faces an impossible task trying to fit the competence, the preferences, the nationality and the politics of the members into a team. Inevitably, since governments' choices reflect the domestic political scene, the Commission turns out to be a "shot-gun coalition" - one that matches the de facto partnership of christian-democrats and social-democrats (with the occasional liberal) to be found in both the Council and the Parliament. The impact of the Commission depends largely on its president - and her/his ability to wield together a team. The influence of individual members will depend on their intellectual capacities (at the weekly one day Commission sessions, members are on their own), their international experience, and the standing of the personal staff whom they appoint.

GATT: together we trade

Trade with the rest of the world was the one area where the member States had no option but to act as a unit and (quite literally) speak with one voice. The Community was based from the start, in 1968, on a "customs union" - the removal of customs barriers and quota restrictions on trade between the member countries. But this also meant all member countries imposing exactly the same duties on imports from the rest of the world: otherwise there would be loopholes which would undermine the customs union. The creation of the customs union of the Six led immediately to a round of negotiations in which non-member countries claimed compensation where they felt that the impact of the common tariff would be more restrictive than the overall effect of the separate national duties Over the years since then there has been a never-ending series of trade talks, under the auspices of GATT (the General Agreement on Tariffs and Trade), with the Commission negotiating on behalf of the Community. It does so flanked by the representatives of the member States, and in close consultation, and its voice carries a great deal of weight. Trade negotiations have often been cited as the best demonstration of the potential power of the Community, as the world's biggest trading unit, when it manages to speak with one voice The Uruguay Round was the exception that very clearly proved the rule. The United States has always been hostile to the Common Agricultural Policy, which it has presented as being excessively protective. The Community, on the other hand, has sought to avoid mixing the quarrel about agricultural protection with negotiations on industrial free trade. For the Uruguay talks the United States were successful

81

in getting the issue of agricultural support on the agenda. In so doing they were in a position to fracture the unity of approach which had made the Community so strong in the past. Divergences of opinion about the Common Agricultural Policy came into the public sphere, with the member of the Commission negotiating on behalf of the Community (Dutchman Hans Andriessen) in conflict with his colleague responsible for the Agricultural Policy (Irishman Ray MacSharry). Andriessen wanted to go further with concessions to the United States, mainly about the level of EC farm support. But MacSharry, speaking for the farm ministers, argued that the reform of the Common Agricultural Policy, adopted in the summer of 1992, was the furthest the Community could go. There was also an open confrontation between the member countries, with the French arguing that the proposed concessions would be disastrous for Community farmers.

With each extension, bringing new countries into the European Community, its relative strength as a trading partner increases. GATT is liable to decline in importance as the Community weaves its web of bilateral agreements, the contents of which it can impose upon its "partners". All of these have a vital interest in access to European markets for their exports, and they are met with solemn promises. But in real terms the Community has no option but to defend its own economy : in the context of a world-wide recession, the Community needs outlets for its own exports, and cannot afford to throw open its own frontiers. GATT thus seems increasingly likely to be an instrument for legalising restrictive trade policies. The only alternative would lie in a fundamental change of stance, with the Community opting for policies based on the principle of maximum self-reliance - for regions within the Community and countries in the world - with trade made subject to tight environmental disciplines. (But this is an approach based on another mode, a building-brick to be laid aside for use when it comes to suggesting a new overall stance for the Community in the world).. This episode, the final outcome of which was repeatedly postponed, showed to what an extent the Community's effectiveness in trade talks had been due to maintaining its internal unity. The message for other aspects of external relations is clear.

GATT's primary function has been to uphold the principle - and the myth - of free trade, which is presented as a vital guarantee of economic growth and development. Inevitably, it is the strongest economies that benefit the most from free trade, which is in reality a guarantee of an economic free-for-all with a minimum of rules. But if GATT leaves the rich countries free to do what they want, and to fight out their quarrels, it also acts as a form of discipline, preventing weaker countries from protecting their economies whilst they strive for a greater degree of autonomy.

The Uruguay round played an important role in demystifying GATT. The official wisdom is that free trade is sacred, and GATT exists to protect it: any return to protection could spell disaster for the world economy. But there is a growing realisation that while GATT is useful in warding off or settling trade conflicts between the main trading countries, it also has another function: that is to impose free trade in situations where it is bound to mean the exploitation of poor countries by their richer trading partners. There was also a new awareness that not only trade looms large in the GATT talks: so do exchanges of services. The developing countries see the GATT rules as bolstering United States domination of the world market in the area of culture and services. The Community is going to have to re-think its stance on these issues.

Farm policy: the exodus and the rake-off

The Common Agricultural Policy, long presented as being the Community's first great success, has turned out to be an albatross round its neck. The avowed aim, written into the Rome Treaty, was to guarantee food supplies - and protect farmers. In practice, it has contributed to the unrelenting process by which small farmers are driven from the land, and at the same time has channelled vast sums - over 60% of the total EC budget - into the coffers of the agro-business (banks, suppliers of agricultural equipment and machinery, food processors....).

That the rural areas whose economy was built around the farming community are dying is not the fault of the CAP (Common Agricultural Policy) alone. The process had already begun, and would have gone on - - if more gradually - without the CAP: it is happening all over the world, not least in the United States. Mechanisation and intensification of farming have brought a fundamental change of attitude, with agriculture treated like any other industry, subject to all-out competition, and unrelenting pressure to increase productivity. Previously, farming differed from other sector because a key factor of production -soil - was unchanging, and another - weather - was unpredictable. Only the farmer's work (and that of his family) and his skill and experience, could make a clear difference in output. So there was not the same pattern of competition as in manufacturing. With tractors and combine harvesters; with artificial fertilisers; more recently with labour-saving machinery and the application of electronics; and finally with bioengineering - it has become possible to achieve a steady increase in yields, or to reduce the amount of land required. The extreme case is that of cattle, pigs, poultry, raised effectively with no land at all: cattle "factories" on the outskirts of Rotterdam, where the cows are fed on soya-cake from the US and never get to graze; chicken "farms" that receive 12,000 chicks a month to fatten them for slaughter). But this trend requires inputs of equipment and capital which make the farmers dependent on the "agri-business" - the big farm banks (the French 'Crédit Agricole' is one of the world's biggest banks) that make them the loans they need to go on expanding; the manufacturers of equipment like fully mechanised cattle-sheds; suppliers of feedstuffs and medicaments for the intensive pig and poultry farms. All this has combined to set in motion a process of concentration in which the smaller farms are ruthlessly eliminated.

It was against this background that the original six EC countries set out, in the 60's, to negotiate a common approach to agricultural trade. The option had little to do with the interests of farmers or consumers: it was part of a basic political deal, whereby the removal of customs opened up French markets to German industry, and in return German markets would be open to French farm produce. (Paradoxically, the end result was to be a vital boost to French industry, and the development of intensive farming in Germany !).

It was decided that the only way to open up agricultural markets, between countries with different farming structures, would be to establish common prices. With the failure of attempts to do this gradually , it was done in one leap, in 1966. But common prices meant fixed prices, and the Community had to undertake a commitment to buy up anything not absorbed by the market. It was this open-ended commitment, to buy whatever was produced and to buy it at a fixed price, that was to be at the root of the CAP disaster. The single price level was very different in its impact on different groups of farmers. For the small farms, with low output, the single price was not enough for them to make a living, whence the steady exodus, while many farming families, with the farmer working a 70 hour week, survived at an income level well below the guaranteed minimum industrial wage.For more dynamic farmers, seeking to keep up with technical progress, the money they could make at the guaranteed price was just enough for them to pay off their debts to the agri-business and stay in the race. Finally, for the big farmers (for instance those with big herds of high-yield milking cows), the guaranteed price was far above their marginal costs. So they were taking a rake-off on every litre they sold, and if they wanted to raise their income had merely to increase the size of their herd, or acquire new land.Support buying at the single Community price was the main reason for the ever-rising cost of the CAP. But it led on to other things. The surpluses which the support commitment encouraged had not only to be bought up, but also disposed of. That meant an item in the Community budget for storage; another for export subsidies as the Community off-loaded onto the world market.(One colourful CAP figure was the flamboyant French dealer, millionaire and card-carrying member of the French Communist party, who negotiated the sale of millions of tonnes of butter to the Soviet Union at reduced rates) Meanwhile in the Community salted butter was doled out to old age pensioners for Christmas.

It was not long before new ways were found to milk the CAP. It became general practice to separate calves from their mothers on birth, so as to benefit from maximum milk output: that milk is sold (for the system continues today) to the dairies, which turn it into skimmed milk powder; and the Community then subsidises a scheme for distributing the milk powder to be mixed with water and fed to the calves, in place of the milk from their mothers. The cost of the operation is measured in milliards of ECUs - but it is "obligatory expenditure" over which the European Parliament has no hold. That makes no allowance, however, for the waste of energy, in transport from farm to dairy to processing plant and back, in the dehydrating process and in storage in the intermediate period. It may be hard to believe: but it is no fairy story, and as long as it is allowed, the farmers will to along with it.

Another story that brings out that the CAP is a hostage of big business concerns isoglucose. As a part of the initial CAP deal, EC producers of sugar-beet (especially the Belgians, who complained that they got a raw deal overall) were allotted quotas far exceeding Community needs; and this competed, both on the Community market and on world markets, with cane sugar from countries where that was a main source of vital foreign currency.At one point in the 70's, a new product made from chemicals came on the market. It was an industrial sweetener, isoglucose. Instead of taxing the new product to prevent it under-cutting the sugar market, the Community introduced a system of support, buying up the isoglucose to protect EC sugar producers.A system that can think up and apply schemes of this kind, and get away with it, need have little fear of reform.

But what has saved the CAP, for a quarter of a century, has been the failure of those who criticised its exorbitant cost to grasp the underlying machinery of open-ended support at a price fixed for all. Two former ministers of agriculture in their respective countries - Edgard Pisani from France and Neil Blaney from Ireland, saw through the scheme, and they have put forward basically the same solution: graduated or multi-tier prices.

The ideas is simple: a minimum amount is bought up at a high enough price to guarantee the survival of the smallest farmers; for a second layer of output a somewhat lower price is guaranteed; and so on, until beyond a certain level there is no subsidy (the farmer is in any case probably competitive on the world market.) A scheme like this has worked in Ireland. But the Commission has never explored the potential of that approach.When there came at last a Commission member for agriculture who wanted to end the rake-off for the big farmers (and thus for the agri lobby), he finally resorted to schemes for taking land out of production, and paying farmers for caring for the land, to cut output by over 20%. But the "reform" fails to cut the overall bill for the CAP, and will certainly fail to stem the disastrous exodus from the land. That the kind of madness incorporated into the CAP should be allowed to bring about the final destruction of rural communities is a sad comment on the values or perhaps of the awareness of both the Eurocrats who run the CAP and the parliaments, national and European, whose priority it ought to be to save the rural culture of Europe...

Regional policy: roads for the isles

An area where the Community has failed, by its own standards, is regional policy. The term is supposed to cover the development of less prosperous areas, and the narrowing (or better still the elimination) of the gaps between the poor and the prosperous areas. Over three decades on from the signing of the Rome Treaty, economic activity is increasingly concentrated in a swathe extending from the south-east of England, via Benelux, the Rhine, the Rhone and northern Italy, known in the jargon as the "blue banana", with a branch across southern France and into Catalonia. The exodus from outlying areas, and from other rural areas where agriculture is in decline, continues with no sign that it can be stopped. Thus the good fortune of some regions matches the doom of others, and the gaps going on getting bigger.

Already in the Rome Treaty, there was the ritual liberal lip-service to the need to narrow gaps between regions. Reference was often made to the Italian experience, where unification had led to a widening of the gap between the industrialised north and the backward, primarily agricultural south. But the sums that the Community was prepared to make available were marginal in relation to the economic forces which made for concentration in already prosperous areas, and the decline of both old industrial and outlying rural areas. The story told by the statistics about regional differences is that the gaps got smaller during the boom years -the overflow of purchasing power and investment capital from the rich to the poorer regions - but widened again in hard times.The same pattern of events seems set to repeat itself. When signing the "Single Act" treaty, which was to do away with the still persisting economic frontiers between member states, and end protected state monopolies, the Twelve gave a token of just how seriously they viewed the likely regional impact: they committed themselves to double the sums the Community would be devoting to regional development. But it is not just the level of funding that counts: it is the kinds of things it is spent on, and the way the problems are tackled.

Not all the regional problems can be laid at the door of the Community. Regions whose economies had been built around traditional industries were facing dramatic decline as a result of world-wide competition. Steel was facing the irresistible challenge of emergent economies (Brazil, Japan); European ship-building could not the competition on a world market with overcapacity; textiles were hit by the efforts of third world producers with lower costs.The policies the Community has followed have been based on two beliefs. One is in investment grants: provided a firm got a big enough launching grant, it could be planted into any economic context and be expected to prosper. The other widely held belief was - and is - in infrastructure: that it suffices to provide ports, airports, and above all roads, to attract an inflow of private sector investment. The results are to be seen in the magnificently engineered but virtually unused roads that head out into the outlying parts of the west of Ireland, or have been bull-dozed out of the cliffs around the Greek islands, to open them up to tourists.

The overall result of existing trends and misplaced Community efforts has been a steady increase in the gaps. A series of developments have made the forces influencing private sector investment policy infinitely more complex, and at the same time made their impact on the regional location of economic activity more powerful.In recent years, fundamental changes have been happening in the organisation of industry. Under the growing pressure of international competition, and the need to cut costs to survive, firms have sought to free the money tied up in stocks and in transport. Assisted by the break-through in communications technology, the big companies operating world wide (automobiles in particular) have organised themselves so that work only begins on a specific product when a new order has been placed. They have also organised their relations with suppliers of parts so that no source is more than a night's truck drive away, and material ordered before the end of the day can be delivered the following morning. Also, the manufacturers have demanded of their suppliers that they become as flexible as possible in adapting to the firm's demands. The end result of all this has been to put plant in outlying areas (which might have been attracted there by investment grants or by the improved infrastructure) at a disadvantage, and to boost the already prosperous areas in which new investment is being concentrated.

What is missing in the story of regional policy is ...the regions. Nor is this by chance. It is another situation where the centralised nation states bear the responsibility for mistaken priorities and missed opportunities. Again there is the lack of openness to a federal approach - aggravated in this case by a jealous determination to prevent direct competition between the regions and the Commission. The bureaucrats in the national capitals were afraid lest the Commission develop its own network of contacts with the regional authorities, which could thus escape the tutelage of the states. The persistence of this attitude was all the more striking because these decades of deadlock have coincided with a trend towards greater power for the regions in certain Community member countries. There are exceptions of course,to the subordinate position of the regions, the most obvious being the Federal Republic of Germany. The state-region of Hamburg, for instance, was one of the first regional governments to establish formal relations with the Commission. Italian regions, too, began to tread a path to the doors of the Commission, but the share-out of Community funding has continued to form the object of squabbling in Rome that left far too high a proportion going on bureaucracy. Even now, the national government must give its formal approval before the President of a region may pay a visit to the Commission. In 1992 when the government went into an austerity phase, to try to bring public sector spending within the norms for being admitted as an active member of Monetary and Economic Union, Rome insisted on cutting back on travel outside Italy , even to the rest of the Community, by regional officials - and in naming the individuals who could or could not travel. So much for regional autonomy...

For many years the Commission failed to take up the struggle to involve regional authorities in contacts at Community level - no doubt because the odds were heavily stacked against it. During the 80's things became less strict, and the Commission openly supported, or even promoted, cooperation between regions. It launched a modest programme of exchange of experience between regions (cautiously limited to technical subjects), and welcomed inter-regional link-ups, such as the grouping of regions from along the Atlantic sea-board, or a link-up of major industrial non-capitals (Milano,

Barcelona...). Not only governments but also lobbies and pressure groups operating at the Community level can be expected to oppose a politicising of the regions that could give them the scope to follow alternative economic policies. For no sector is this truer than for energy. It happens to be the outlying areas of the Community that have the biggest potential for meeting their energy needs from renewable sources : all down the Atlantic sea-board a changing combination of wind power, tidal power, wave power, and short-rotation forestry; around the Mediterranean, solar energy above all, combined in places with wind energy. It was predictable that national energy utilities, producing and selling electricity from oil or from nuclear power stations, would do all in their power to put the brake on such developments. As we shall see in looking for a Community energy policy, there has been no overall approach to such inter-acting and over-lapping issues.

Just how little regions enter into the concerns of the central governments of the Community is well illustrated by the Maastricht Treaty. The Twelve agreed to create, for the first time in the history of the Community, a " Committee of the Regions" - on the face of it a major step towards recognising a role for the regions. But... the Committee is given the same status as the Economic and Social Committee, set up by the Rome Treaty back in 1957, to take account of the views of employers' organisations, trade unions, and representatives of the "general interest" (e.g. farmers, the professions). Being forced to aim at consensus, it has never carried weight with the ministers or the Commission. It is not an official organ of the Community and has no right to take initiatives. The Maastricht Treaty actually promoted the Court of Auditors to the status of "organ of the Community" but left the new Committee aligned on the ESC. If there had been any real desire to give the Committee of the Regions weight, its members would have been designated, or better still elected, by the regions. Instead, ultimate irony, they are to be appointed by the national governments, with no obligation to consult the regions.

But the Community is not going to escape the regional issue. One reason is economic. There is every sign, as we have seen, that certain central areas will increasingly attract economic activity : the "blue banana" is becoming a reality. And at the same time, the decline in rural areas continues, under pressure from the forced exodus of farmers. The other reason is constitutional: the inter-action of Community and regional responsibilities. On the one hand, with the enlargement of its competence, the Community finds itself adopting measures in areas for which, under national constitutions, the regions not the nation states have the right of decision.

Thus the German "Länder" (regions) have always had responsibility for forestry policy, and Community measures applying to forestry, agriculture, and regions can clash with this. The Länder are also responsible for education, an area into which the Community formally moves with the provisions of the Single Act. The Germans have been seeking a pragmatic formula to enable the Länder to have their views put in the Council. Likewise, in Belgium education is a matter for Flanders, Wallonia and the Brussels conurbation, each of which has a minister in charge in its regional government, and no chance of one agreeing to be represented by another.

The other way around, Community work on environmental policy is a source of problems in Spain, where as part of devolution built into the post-Franco constitution, the autonomous regions have sole responsibility for the environment. There is a vast potential in regional autonomy for combating the increase in gaps between regions - but on condition that the central governments are prepared to allow regional authorities to make their own choices. The inter-acting complex of regions/energy/agriculture/tourism is a good example. Few of the nation states are likely to devote a major part of their investment effort to renewable energies - the electricity industry based on nukes and on oil will see to that. But there are regions which could switch to bio-mass (energy crops), and wind, wave and tidal power to give their industries the advantage of cheaper energy costs, and provide a wave of jobs in research production, maintenance and export of renewable energy sources.

Energy: the policy that never was

In any investigation, what is not there is often as revealing as what is. If the European Community, after four decades, has still no overall energy policy - nor even a binding commitment to seek one - there must be an explanation. Energy is, after all, a crucial element in the economy. There is a direct relationship between energy and employment: automation, and more recently robotisation, are ways of substituting other forms of energy for human effort. The same is true of the new revolution which is replacing mental effort (from calculation through to design) by computer programmes. There are also implications for employment in the possible options about energy supply. The dominant techniques of energy supply, which use oil, gas or nuclear energy to fuel power stations producing electricity, use a minimum of labour. By contrast, techniques which involve using small de-centralised units drawing on renewable energy source - solar heating (passive or photovoltaic), wind turbines,.. - are relatively labour intensive in their production, installation and maintenance.

Options about energy production and end use can have an influence in terms of economic centralisation or de-centralisation. Thus giant electric power stations, providing cheap energy for areas where economic activity is concentrated, will exercise a centralising pull on the economy, whereas small-scale renewable energy projects can help to provide a basis for regional autonomy. Certain forms of energy are harmful to the environment: coal and gas adding to the CO_2 problem, nuclear power with the risk of accidents and damage by radiation. Others - solar, wind, wave or geothermic energy - are eco-friendly   Finally, there is an important strategic aspect to energy supply. Guaranteeing access to the energy supplies on which an economy has chosen to rely is one of the over-riding motivations for foreign policy, and even for military action, in today's world. It is a commonplace that guaranteeing access to Middle East oil sources has determined the policies of the industrialised countries in the area.

It might therefore be expected that the Community would have set out from the start to develop an overall energy policy, seeking the best pattern of energy supply and use, in the light of these and other elements. Such a policy would weigh the arguments about the whole complex range of forms of energy: solar energy (passive and photovoltaic); wind power; tidal energy; wave power; short rotation forestry feeding small power stations; marine heat exchangers; geo-thermic heat sources and "hot rock" techniques; hydro-electric power; coal; natural gas; oil in all its forms; nuclear power (fission); and power from An explanation of why this did not happen should give some indications - though probably no proofs - about how it can be as important for some vested interests and lobbies to prevent the Community from acting as it is for others to ensure that it acts - and acts in ways from which they benefit. The lack of a coherent energy policy, independent of outside pressures, may have cost the Community vital decades in developing the potential of forms of energy that are compatible with responsible and non-destructive economic development.

In the late '60s, when the Rome Treaty establishing the European Economic Community was being negotiated, belief in nuclear power as a reliable and inexhaustible source of cheap energy was at its peak. Just as pooling coal resources under the Coal and Steel Community had been seen as a guarantee of peace, so pooling know-how and resources in the nuclear power field would help to weld the Community together. A separate

91

Community, called Euratom, was established. As it happened, de Gaulle did not see it that way, and preferring to use nuclear power as a basis for French autonomy, he despatched a top diplomat to Brussels, as president of the Euratom Commission, with a mandate to sabotage the ambitions of its founders. The job was efficiently done, and Euratom finished up doing little more than finance research - quite a lot of it on nuclear safety. One of the results of the existence of Euratom was that when the three Communities (Coal and Steel, Euratom and EC) were merged, the department dealing with energy was dominated by the nuclear energy lobby, which worked to ensure that the nuclear industry got a maximum of funds from the Community budget - and that renewable energy was neglected on the grounds that it was "not yet competitive". Cynically, the Community was left with the task of researching into nuclear safety - an odd priority given the lobby case that nuclear power is perfectly safe... In the Commission administration, nuclear and oil interests set the tone, and dominated the energy department. Renewable energy (and techniques of energy saving) have been dealt with only by a tiny unit within the Research department. Not allowed to finance pilot projects, they concentrated on bringing together researchers from all over the Community, to pool their results and maximise the impact of their work. One of their many successes was a breakthrough in spreading techniques for using "hot rocks" (deep hot layers used to heat circulating water).

But the way the scales were weighted against renewable energy is illustrated by the story of wave power. In the 70's a scheme devised by wave power pioneer Prof. Salter, using big concrete caissons rolling with the waves - " Salter's ducks"- was at the stage where it would have benefitted from independent financing.It was a scheme that besides having a major potential for meeting electricity requirements at a lower cost (and thus querying the relative appeal of nuclear power), also opened up the prospect of long-term contracts for ship-yards in Ulster (Northern Ireland) suffering from the collapse of the ship-building industry and the run-down of the oil-rig business. But pressure from the UK government prevented the Commission from setting aside even the kind of limited support being granted for other forms of renewable energy. The UK government's energy research centre at Aldermaston, essentially concerned with nuclear energy, published figures purporting to show that wave power was far more costly per unit of energy produced than nuclear power. It was nearly a decade before the truth was leaked: that the Aldermaston figures were wrong, and had been used intentionally to block support for wave power; wave power from Salter's "ducks" was potentially far cheaper than nuclear power. Even then, the Commission's proposals for research funding continued to leave out wave power.

There is a striking contrast between the Community' failure to come up with an overall proposal on energy, and the rapid progress that has been made, since the changes of the last few years in central and eastern Europe (including the former USSR), in working out an "Energy Charter". This is a pact covering the future exploitation of energy resources, particular on the territory of the former Soviet Union. By contrast with its traditional stance of seeking to have the Community as such take part in international agreements of all kinds, the member States have been quite willing to take part separately in this new undertaking.

It seems reasonable to make a guess that the Commission's reluctance to press for a single overall energy policy, and the member States readiness to adopt a totally non-Community framework for developing the vast energy resources of what was the Soviet Union, reflect the strategies of the oil and nuclear lobbies. Neither the giant oil companies nor the nuclear energy producers (constructors and operators of reactors) have any interest in transparency as regards present and future costs of energy from different sources. That could hardly fail to show that renewable energies, besides being safer and more eco-friendly, are also either presently or potentially competitive, particularly in relation to nuclear energy. It would also inevitably bring out the scope for breaking with dependence on oil imported from strategically precarious areas. If the factual bases were to be laid for a Community (or still more a Europe-wide) energy policy, it could not fail to challenge the tight grip that the oil and nuclear lobbies hold over national patterns of energy production and consumption.

The renewable energy unit in the Commission's research department has for the last decade and a half had available on data base the figures needed to simulate energy scenarios and identify optimum patterns of energy production and use. That fact that it has not chosen to do so can reliably be put down to the success of the lobbies in freezing debate, and the success of oil and nuke propaganda about the costs and lack of competitivity of the whole range of renewable energies. Yet anyone who cares to put together even the down-beat figures available, about the proportions of the energy market which the various renewable sources could supply - even without any increase in the scale of investment - cannot fail to admit that alternative scenarios need to be taken seriously. What this brings out is the need for the Commission to adopt an independent stance. But for that to happen there would have to be

Commission member with a commitment to independence, the courage to stand up to the lobbies, and the weight needed to win over the Commission to providing whole-hearted support...

Environment: who is winning ?

When the European Community came into being, in 1958, awareness of environmental problems was at its beginnings. You will look in vain, in the Rome Treaty, for anything about the environment - am omission that reflects the situation at that time in the Community generally.

When the issue began to be publicly recognised,in the early 1970s, the Community institutions were slow to take it up. On the contrary, the issue was planted like a long-maturing cuckoo's egg in the nest of the Commission, led at that time by former French Eurocrat François-Xavier Ortoli. The European Parliament - not yet directly elected - began to take up the environmental issue, and found a partner in the Commission which set up a small special unit, responsible directly to the Commission, to work on environmental problems. It was headed by a high-powered and ambitious French Eurocrat, Michel Carpentier.

One of Carpentier's first moves was to conjure up a Community-level body, the European Environment Bureau, bringing together non-governmental organisations in the field, to engage in a dialogue with the Commission and give its proposals the necessary legitimacy (a form of benign manipulation in which only a few organisations refused on principle to get involved). There was to be no shortage of issues. Environmental action groups realised that air and water pollution were no respecters of national boundaries, and were disappointed at their governments' slowness in responding to popular concern.

It was a natural reaction to turn to the Community, and especially from 1979 onwards, once it was directly elected, to the European Parliament. This they did, with demands for action over issues as varied as the destruction of forests by acid rain or the fate of baby seals at the hands of heartless Newfoundland hunters: faced with a heap of a million and more letters and postcards, dumped outside the chamber in Strasbourg, MEPs could not fail to recognise that the seal pups were an issue that their constituents cared about.

Lacking a specific legal basis for proposals for Community legislation, the Commission had recourse to the portmanteau article 130, which allows for any proposals that are in the best interests of the Community - but requires unanimous voting. Before long the Commission managed to start regular meetings of the Council on environmental issues. But at that time hardly any member countries had ministers for the environment - and where they did exist they tended to be at the bottom of the pecking order in their national governments.

The first steps had been made on the way to a Community environmental policy - but it was not going to be an easy road to follow. Initially, the Commission's approach appeared to be haphazard. This was essentially because it had to give priority to responding to the most pressing events or problems. Thus the explosion at the Seveso chemical plant in northern Italy, followed not long afterwards by an accident at the Sandoz chemicals plant on the Rhine near Basle, led to pressures for proposals about waste disposal and safety measures in the chemicals industry. The revelation of a series of scandals about toxic waste being transported illegally from one country to another - from Germany where the rules on disposal were strict to France where they were lax - led to a directive in that area of policy. Considerably effort went into having the Community as a unit, rather than national countries acting separately, take part in key international Conventions on matters such as preservation of species or pollution of the seas.

Within the Commission environment had acquired the status of a fully-fledged department (DG X), and was the primary responsibility of one Member. But it tended to be seen as one of the poor relations (for long the status of Social Affairs), near the bottom of the list when jobs were being shared out in each new Commission. DG XI with a small staff, found itself (and to this day still finds itself) repeatedly up against the might of the Department for Industry, one of the biggest and strongest departments, and always with a heavy-weight Commissioner (the top Belgian diplomat Etienne Davignon, the British industrialist Lord Cockfield, followed by the former German minister for economics, Martin Bangemann).

Nevertheless, the tide was running the right way. The Single Act, taking effect in 1988, was mainly concerned with providing the legal basis for removing the remaining economic barriers to the single market: but it was also the first text to recognise environmental issues. It laid down (in a new Art.100(a) that certain environmental proposals relevant to the single market could be decided in the Council by majority voting, whilst others - purely environmental - would continue to require a unanimous vote in the Council (Art.130 S). This made the choice of the legal basis for proposals a delicate one. The Commission frequently clashed with the Parliament, whose

Environment Committee wanted on principle to insist that issues were purely environmental (130) whereas the Commission saw using Art.100(a) and a majority vote as being more likely to yield the desired results.

The Maastricht Treaty took things a step further, extending majority voting to environmental issues as such. Art. 130S(1) provides for decision by majority after a "concertation" procedure and two readings, whereas Art. 130S/2 specifies areas still requiring unanimity after a single reading. These include such broad issues as land use, management of water resources, and energy policy choices. Once the general thrust of policy has been laid down in that way, then measures within the defined framework can be decided by majority voting.

Weightier problems emerge when an issue arises on which some member States already apply stricter norms than are being proposed for the Community. In general, it is the richer northern countries that have high standards, whereas the southern countries say that an immediate tightening of the rules would price their industries to extinction. A specific case of major economic significance came to the surface in 1993: it concerned measures to recuperate packaging waste. The Commission had tabled a draft directive allowing for the fact that it will take time for countries in the south to come into line with those in the north. But Germany, Denmark and the Netherlands were already applying stricter rules, which they could not be expected to abandon. As provided for in the Maastricht Treaty, the draft directive provided for member States wishing to maintain stricter norms to do so. But under the terms of the interpretation from the Commission's legal service, there is a double condition: that the text be adopted by majority vote, and that the States in question either voted against or abstained. The three countries with tighter legislation felt they were obliged to vote against the draft directive, in order to be free to maintain their own national systems, while the measure adopted would put pressure on the southern countries to raise their standards within a 5-year time limit. To make things more difficult still, Germany was criticised for applying norms that were producing more used packaging than its processing industry could handle - and exporting it to other member States where it flooded their infant industry and prevented them from meeting the norms in the directive.

The Community has also taken on some of the big issues, where even more is at stake. DG XI has sought to further the idea of a CO_2 tax, to be levied on fuels that contribute to the levels of CO_2 in the atmosphere; but it has run into opposition inside the Commission itself, as well as from outside. The final Commission decision depends above all on the judgement of the member responsible for tax policy, the former MEP Christian Scrivener, and with the national ministers concerned. Against that alliance, the environment department packs little punch.

The hard fact is that environmental considerations are nowhere near the top of the political priority list, be it for the Commission itself or the national governments. There are innumerable pointers that bring this out. As President of the Commission Jacques Delors regularly made policy speeches in which he recalls the broad sweep of the Commission's concerns. In many cases, there is little or no reference to the environment; in others, it is mentioned, but not as a priority.The Commission's stance over attendance at the World Environmental Summit in Rio in 1992 was significant. The Council of Ministers of the Environment having failed to achieve a positive Community position on reduction of CO2 emissions, the member responsible for the environment, the Italian Socialist former MEP Carlo Ripa di Meano, decided that he would emphasise their failure and his disappointment by not attending the opening session. Delors, on the other hand, went to Rio, thus undermining Ripa di Meano's gesture and revealing that he saw his representing the Community at a session of world heads of government to be more important than the issue of substance.

As is so often the case over the environment it is hard to conclude whether the battle is being won or lost. True, there are more and more Community directives, clamping down on the worst abuses, building up a body of law that will also be extended to the other, non-EC, countries in the European Economic Area. But on the other hand, there continue to be scandals - about illegal transport and dumping of waste. On the positive side must be counted the clean-up of bathing beaches, but irreversible pollution of the Mediterranean and of the Baltic continue unabated. The Community as such has finally joined the Convention on Threatened Species - but throughout Europe asphalt, concrete and industrial buildings continue to encroach on the countryside and spell the inexorable disappearance of species of flowers, birds, and insects and of mammals like foxes, badgers or otters. The massive hand-outs to the weaker economies, which were used to oil the passage of the Maastricht Treaty, were destined in part for the building of many more thousands of miles of motorways: the figure going around was 12,000 km - seven thousand five hundred miles - of new motorways. In the Delors white paper on ways out of the economic crisis, produced at the end of 1993, the same figure recurred. Even if does not mean that twice as many miles of concrete are to be laid, it does add to the evidence of the Community's lack of real concern about the environment.

In short, now as twenty years ago the situation at the Community level reflects the ambiguity that reigns at the national level. Many years will pass before the senior post after the President of the Commission is that of member responsible for environment, or the department for environment has worked itself out of a job because all other departments automatically take environmental concerns fully into account and all measures are vetted for environmental impact, at the planetary as well as the Community level.

8 Un-parliament

The European Parliament is like a luxury cruise liner. From time to time it returns to port, the crew get a well-earned holiday, and many of the passengers go ashore, to be replaced by others. Then it sets sail again - in the case of the EP for as long as five years.There is much waving of flags, and giving of interviews: but before the floating palace has even sunk beneath the horizon, its existence has been forgotten. On board, however, the passengers rapidly get absorbed in shipboard activities, which come to seem increasingly important: committee meetings, amendments to Community legislation, "inter-groups" where those concerned about animal welfare, or who have their constituencies on the Atlantic coast-line, or who lobby for nuclear or renewable energy, get together across political party lines...

And when news comes in of events in distant corners of the world, they send out messages of condemnation or congratulation, the wording of which is discussed over and over and many times revised. Tyrants all over the planet are bombarded with injunctions from the European Parliament to commute death penalties and respect human rights. But in the land from which the voyagers set off, there are few who recall the cruise at all.

Once a month, on the stroke of five on a Monday afternoon, an usher in black tails and white bow-tie cries " El Presidente" (or the equivalent in any one of eight languages), and the two hundred or so members scattered around the European Parliament hemicycle, beneath the dramatic sweep of its sombre red-pine roof, rise briefly to their feet as the President enters, takes his seat, and declares open the proceedings of the next part session.

Then begins a lively hour devoted mainly to the Parliament's programme for the short week until it rises again at the end of Friday morning, but serving also the useful function of letting Members raise (or try to) anything under the sun - usually with the idea of showing their constituents that they, the Members, haven't forgotten them. Observing the ritual, even an experienced watcher could be excused for being taken in, and seeing this as really a Parliament - not a role-playing game for 560 players aged from 21 to 85...This may sound unkind to the vast majority of EP members who take their job seriously, and the Parliament's dedicated staff. But it will certainly not serve the cause of a genuinely democratic Community set-up, at some point in the future, to hush-up the shortcomings of the present gathering, which is elected on a totally distorted basis, has no real powers, and plays none of the roles normally filled by a parliament.

In point of fact, it is the situation instituted by the governments in 1979 that has something cruelly cynical about it. That was when the heads of government, meeting as the European Council, decreed that the Parliament should be directly elected by universal suffrage. On the face of it, they seemed to be remedying what had been for a quarter of a century the major weakness of the Community system - the lack of a meaningful parliament. Here was an occasion to enhance that democracy to which they were so deeply committed,and which had divided them from the socialist countries throughout the decades of the Cold War. But in fact they were to reveal their underlying lack of respect for parliaments.

On the face of it, there was going to be, for the first time, a body which could control the bureaucrats in Brussels, and the ministers, meeting behind closed doors, who were taking more and more decisions which affected the lives of citizens in the member countries. Some naively, some cynically, some resignedly because they had concluded that even a limping "parliament" not worthy of the name had the potential to carve out a role for itself, the politicians of the Community countries went along with the charade.But if the citizens believed they were being given a parliament, they were the victims of a European level confidence trick. What the heads of government needed was a democratic alibi for the activities of the European Council, that club of prime ministers (plus the French president), which had begun to meet three or four times a year and settle (or not) all the major issues in the Community. The "Parliament", though directly elected, was to have no more powers than the gathering of delegations from national parliaments that had preceded it.

Twenty-five years before, when the six founder members set up the first European Community, with a mandate limited to the affairs of the coal and steel sectors, its executive body was the "High Authority", which had certain direct powers, with which the governments of the member countries could not interfere. This might have been thought to merit direct democratic control. But the governments of the time baulked at that hurdle. They were not prepared to let the democratic cat out of the inter-governmental bag.They wrote into the ECSC Treaty the possibility of an elected assembly, but then opted for a second degree body, with members delegated from national parliaments In 1967, when the European Economic Community was set-up, there was no change as regards democratic control. It inherited the same delegated body, and the few members who out of "European" conviction took their Euro-mandate seriously soon learned that they had forfeited any chances at home, and even ran the risk of being penalised by their constituents for neglecting their national responsibilities.

Inevitably, the first direct elections aroused many hopes and illusions. The fact that they were in reality a set of parallel national elections, for national contingents that would come together to make up a Euro-Parliament, did little to dampen the enthusiasm - but did effectively rule out that shake-up that might have been expected if there had been Community-wide lists facing each other under a single electoral system.The joint electoral platforms that had been worked out by Europe-wide conferences of Socialists, Christian-Democrats, Liberals or Communists, all with their fine-sounding principles, mostly stayed piled in the corridors in Brussels. Instead, the national party machines swung into action, trotting out essentially the same old faces and the same issues, and insisting that this must be seen as another important test of their party's strength, or a vote of confidence in the government in power. In countries with proportional representation and electoral lists, there was hardly a major party whose leader did not head his party's European list. So for a brief moment, the first elected parliament seemed to be a historic gathering of leading politicians from the Community countries. But the spell was not to last long. The governments had made sure that there would be no unpleasant surprises, by declining to make any changes in the powers of the Parliament. So there was nothing to attract the big names, which were soon off back to the realities of the national political game, which offered the prospect of power - albeit it within limits.

Meanwhile, the proceedings of the Parliament's first session did not augur well in terms of attachment to democracy - though they did give an unexpected and unplanned glimpse of issues which the political establishments would rather let go by in silence. For the best part of that first week-long session, the efforts of the main political parties were concentrated on an effort to prevent the duly elected representatives of minority parties from obtaining the right to defend their interests on an equal footing. By a nice twist of historic irony, it turned out that the oldest Member, to whom fell the honour of opening the first session of the first directly-elected European Parliament, was one of the historic figures of Gaullisme. Eighty-two-year-old Louise Weiss was a Resistance heroine, who continued to believe fervently in the General's vision of a Europe of the fatherlands ('Europe des patries'), and it was of this she spoke at length, rather than the federal Europe which for many of those present was the goal to which the elected Parliament was to be a vital step.

When Ms Weiss finished speaking, it was her job to move at once to the election of a President for the Parliament. But she used her prerogative to call a series of speakers who were sitting grouped together in the back row of the chamber, - in the mountains as they call it in the Italian parliament.

The first to be called was Emma Bonino, from the Radical Party in Italy, who protested at the "five per cent clause" in Germany. Written into the post-war German constitution, the hurdle which required a party to get 5% of the votes cast before being entitled to a seat had been intended to avoid the proliferation of small parties that had undermined the Weimar Republic in the 1920's: but applied to Germany in the context of a Community-wide election, it was patently an effort to clip the wings of minority parties - in this case the emergent German "Greens" - who might link up to achieve an impact at the European level. And indeed the Grünen, though inexperienced and facing largely hostile media coverage, had picked up 943,000 votes in the Federal Republic - a score which should have brought them 2 seats. But thanks to the 5% cut-off they got none.

A second speaker, Luciana Castellina from the extreme left Party of Proletarian Unity for Communism (PDUP), a splinter group from the Italian Communist party, switched attention to France, challenging the mandates of the 81 French members. Determined to keep out marginal elements, the predominant French parties had manoeuvred even more than the French, importing the 5% clause with no justification, switching to national lists to rule out constituency-level surprises, and imposing an impossible financial handicap on small parties. So the ecologists, with 4.6% of the votes, got none of the four seats they should have been entitled to; the left-wing Workers' Struggle ("Lutte Ouvrière") was denied the two seats it should have been entitled to; centrists and extreme right were also deprived of a likely two seats each...

With their captive audience unable to stop them, others joined in to strengthen the indictment. They recalled that the parties present in the out-going delegated assembly had allotted themselves public money to campaign with, and denied it to all others, thus compounding injustice. They pointed

102

the finger at the United Kingdom, where the use of the constituency system meant that the Liberals, though winning no less than 13% of the votes,had not a single seat in Strasbourg. They reminded the Parliament that hundreds of thousands of Italian migrant workers had not been able to vote.

With this salvo of protest on behalf of the disenfranchised, the directly-elected Parliament was off to a start which did it credit. But that was not how it looked to the political establishment, and particularly to the clique who had run the affairs of the old assembly. But they found themselves hoist with their own petard. Their control over the assembly had relied on the system of "political groups". The groups, consisting of members from the main political families (Christian-Democrats, Socialists, Liberals, Gaullists, Conservatives and Communists), had reserved all the spoils for themselves: speaking time, the pick of seats and spots in the parliamentary committees, and funds and facilities (such as meetings with interpretation during one week per month) for themselves. The disturbing newcomers - not just the Radical Party or the Italian far left, but minority parties from other countries - must be excluded from this at all costs.

But like many a dominant majority before them, they had underestimated their opponents. In the six-week period between the elections and the first session, the minority parties became aware that they risked being treated as second-class members in the new Parliament. To resist, they would have to get together. In this they were helped by an unusual group that had grown up in Brussels, with its network of political contacts in most European countries, under the name agenor. Growing up around a limited circulation magazine, agenor had been acting for years as an informal think-tank and communications group, and was known and trusted by most of the minority parties. Members of the group were able to help them overcome the barriers of language and political method that would otherwise have prevented them acting together. At a meeting in Luxembourg, before the July session, the minority parties agreed to take advantage of the Rules of the Parliament. These said that any ten members, provided they came from at least four countries, could establish a political group "on a basis of affinity". The affinity was not difficult to establish: the defence of their democratic rights. Meanwhile, the established groups were trying to block this loop-hole. Using the formal ruling body of the outgoing assembly, they drafted a change in the rules to raise the 10-member, four-country hurdle, and decided to force it through the new Parliament.

That was to under-estimate the potential of the outsiders in terms of parliamentary resistance tactics. Under the Rules the new Group, with the cautiously descriptive but nevertheless provocative title "Group for the Coordination and Defence of Independent Groups and Members", came into being automatically when Ms. Weiss received formal notification of its creation, which she did in the opening seconds of the new Parliament, whilst duly informing the assembly.

The "TCDI" was to waste no time in using its prerogatives as a Group, starting a procedural guerrilla that was to occupy the Parliament, to the exclusion of almost all else, for the first four days of its existence. And every stage of the filibuster was calculated to wrong-foot the majority. First came the elections. A neat deal had been done, behind the scenes, to ensure the unopposed election of Ms Simone Weil, a French Liberal and former health minister - but with no parliamentary experience. In exchange, the Christian-Democrats were to get the presidency half-way through the five-year life of the Parliament, and the British placed a former National Farmers' Union president as chair of the key Agricultural Committee. By running Emma Bonino for President, the TCDI garnered just enough votes to force a second ballot - and take up half a day. The tactic was repeated next day for the election of the vice-presidents.

Then came the adoption of the agenda, with the old guard seeking to put the vital Rules change, which would have wiped out the TCDI, before even the setting up of committees. They succeeded, but not before the TCDI had used its prerogative as a Group to call for three roll-call votes (each, in those old days before the arrival of electronic voting, taking up two hours, as Members names were called and they queued to put their voting papers in a single urn. When the report was finally tabled, the Parliament was faced with no less than 5000 draft amendments to the Rules - the Radical Party's own special contribution to the filibuster - on which it could not vote until they had been translated into all the official languages. At three o'clock on the Friday morning, with Danish social-democrats indignantly refusing to accept anything not in their mother tongue (especially something that would damage their anti-Market follow members...) the establishment caved in, and accepted a truce in order to be able to set up its committees and start work. The rebels finally won in October, when the bid to vote them out of existence was abandoned, and the story has long since faded into the collective sub-conscious of the Parliament. But it has its political significance. By creating a bridgehead, and holding it, the TCDI Group was acting in the interests of minorities of all kinds. Without this victory the green parties, who first won seats in the second round of Euro-elections in 1984, would probably have been denied Group status. Instead, they were able to join forces with the regionalists and the Danish anti-Marketeers to constitute the Rainbow Group, which guaranteed all three partners access to the full range of Group rights and facilities.This in turn opened the way for the green and green left parties to form their own group in the 1989 parliament while the regionalists and the Danish People's Movement against EC membership stayed together and kept the name of Rainbow Group.

Even with the move to direct elections, the national governments did nothing to increase the powers of the Parliament. On the Parliament side, many factors militated against any immediate confrontation on this key issue. Many members were new not just to the European parliament, but to elected office, and almost all of them were busy coming to grips with operating in the demanding multi-lingual context of the Community. The federalist old-timers realised that in any case public opinion would expect the elected Parliament to use the powers it already had, though hopefully with the enhanced weight and effectiveness that would derive from its new-found legitimacy.

Budget testing ground

The testing ground, for seeing if the elected Parliament packed a bigger punch, would be the procedure for the adoption of the Community budget. The Parliament had acquired, over the years, a say in that procedure : the draft budget for the Community, drawn up by the Commission, was submitted to the Parliament for a first reading - and amendments - before going to the Council of Ministers. As a general rule, the Parliament tends to want increased spending, and the Council is restrictive. Expenditure proposed by the Parliament in first reading, then chopped by the Council, can be restored in second reading if voted by an absolute majority, and the Council can then only cut it again if it is unanimous. At the end of the line it is the President of the Parliament who on receiving the version that emerges from Council declares, on her or his own authority, that the budget is adopted.

There are several problems which make Parliament's role less important and less real than it might seem. The first is that it has no say over what is known as the "compulsory expenditure" under the Common Agricultural Policy (any more than does the Council of Ministers, at least during the budgetary procedure). That is the spending on farm subsidies - intervention to buy up, stock-pile and dispose of surpluses, including export rebates - which makes up most of the farm policy budget, and over 60% of the total

Community budget. This spending depends on a series of factors over which neither the Parliament nor the Council of Finance Ministers has control : the prices set by the Council of Ministers of Agriculture; climatic conditions and market trends, which determine the amounts produced; and the measures thought up to try to reduce the surpluses.

It is one of the many paradoxes of the Community's half-way situation that the Council of Ministers constitutes, under the Treaties, a single body; but that in practice the Agricultural Council and the Finance Council consist of different ministers, and have different and often conflicting policies. One of the reasons for the creation of the "European Council" at heads of government level was the need to arbitrate in such cases.

The second weakness from which the Parliament suffers emerged clearly in the early years after the direct elections. The Parliament decided to challenge the Council head on, and its President refused to sign the budget as approved by the Council. The Parliament has in fact a margin within which it can claim an increase in the budget, and the dispute turned on the Council's restrictive interpretation of this. In the event of a deadlock over the budget, the Community does not grind to a halt, but spending may only continue on a month-by-month basis, each time with a ceiling of one-twelfth of the previous year's expenditure. Initially, the main victim was the Commission. But by the summer, concern was growing about what would happen when there were not the necessary funds available to cover farm policy expenditure. This prospect provided a real deadline for concluding the new round of budgetary procedure, and the Parliament was forced to conclude after obtaining less than it could have done in the closing stages of the original procedure. Both sides saved face by sending their dispute to the Court of Justice for a ruling.

The following year, the Parliament adopted subtler tactics, juggling with figures to yield a major increase in its permitted margin of extra spending. Since then, though relations between the Parliament and the Council over the budget remain tense, the Parliament has accepted that it has nothing to gain from seeking to impose its will on the Council, and the centre of interest has shifted to the "concertation" procedure which takes place before the second reading of the budget in the Council.

This is in fact one of the few times when the Parliament gives the impression of being "real". The Budget Committee has in any case got a different feel about it from the other parliamentary committees: its members from the different political groups are linked by a feeling of solidarity that comes from the fact that they fight together for the Parliament against the

Council, rather than against each other in the traditional party line-ups. During the budgetary procedure, a delegation consisting of one the President of the Budget Committee and one Member from each political group, but led by the President of the Parliament, engages in negotiations with the Council. The junior finance ministers (secretaries of state in most countries), led by their colleague from the country currently holding the presidency of the Council, faces the Parliament's delegation. The meetings, more often than not going on late into the night, in a room packed with concerned officials and many parliamentarians, can involve tough and even dramatic clashes. One of these occasions was when Pierre Pflimlin, prime minister of France during the tense time when de Gaulle returned to power, was President of the Parliament, and did not mince his words in criticising the members of the Council for their lack of vision. The Parliament's delegation returns at each stage to report to the Budget Committee and get its support for the pursuit of the negotiations.

Once it became clear that the scope for enlarging the Parliament's power in the budgetary sphere was in fact limited, interest switched to the case for a change in its role overall, in the framework of political union. The pressure for this came above all from Altiero Spinelli, one of the last remaining "gurus" of the movement for unification. A former Communist who endured twenty years in Fascist prisons, including long years when he was boycotted by fellow prisoners after quitting the party over the Stalin purges, he was the author of a call for a federal Europe, drafted whilst still in prison, at Ventotene, in 1944. In the post war period he had led the campaign of the federalists in Italy for direct elections to a constituent assembly for the Community. Forced to abandon this as unrealistic, he had tried working from within the Community institutions, accepting a post as member of the European Commission responsible for industrial policy. With the arrival of direct elections, he agreed to stand as an independent on the list of the Italian Communist Party. In the Parliament he fought for and obtained the creation of an Institutional Committee, of which he himself was chairperson.He also created a cross-party informal group of those MEPs committed to a federal Europe - insensitively called the "Crocodile" after the extremely expensive Strasbourg restaurant where it held its meetings.But although he managed to get the Parliament to draft and adopt a proposed Treaty of Political Union, the initiative fell victim to the "European trap" : in the attempt to win across-the-board support, the text had been stripped of any political content. As a result, many MEPs on the left felt unable to vote for it - among them the more left-wing members of the German Social Democrats.

Spinelli's Treaty met with competition from more "realistic" but cautious texts, in particular one proposed by a former Italian foreign minister, Emilio Colombo, and the Federal German Liberal foreign minister Horst Genscher. But it was to be overtaken, above all, by the institutional tinkering which the governments set in motion in parallel with the Community's new initiative: the single market. The Parliament had in fact little say in working out the changes in its powers and procedures which formed one of the components of the Single Act. These undoubtedly do reinforce, slightly, the Parliament's position. For proposed Community legislation in certain areas - the creation of the single market, by the removal of economic barriers, on the one hand; and environmental issues (plus some social issues) on the other - a two-reading procedure was introduced. Providing an amendment to the Commission's proposal obtained an absolute majority in first reading, the Parliament could re-instate it on second reading, and the Council only reject it unanimously. But once again, things were not as attractive as they seemed, On the one had, the system left the Council a let-out: there was nothing to compel it to act on a Commission proposal, so in the event of parliamentary amendments unacceptable to a majority in the Council, the latter would just have to pigeon-hole it, and the parliament's attempt to impose its view would be frustrated. There was also a more political result of the new system: it means, in practice, that to obtain the required majority on first reading, amendments must have the support of two biggest political groups - the socialists and the christian-democrats. There is thus an incentive to them to reach a compromise on anything at all controversial - after which their respective allies have little option but to toe the line. Thus the prospect of a political confrontation, that will make it clear for public opinion what the issue is about, and what divides the various groups, is tacitly ruled out. Thus a provision officially intended to strengthen the power of the Parliament contributes in practice to imposing the domination of the "Grand Coalition" of social-democrats and christian democrats. Both groups are happy to maintain an informal alliance, while for time to time invoking solidarity with their smaller partners (the Socialists with the two Communist groups, the Greens and the Rainbow Group; the Christian Democrats with the Liberals, Conservatives and Gaullists) where it suits the political image they want to project.

One reason why this can happen is that the Parliament does not in fact play any of the three main possible roles for a parliament. The role it comes nearest to is that of legislature: after all, texts due to acquire force of law throughout the Community are submitted to it, and can be amended or rejected. For some policy areas, as we have seen, there is a first- and second-reading procedure, which enables the Parliament to exert its influence: but the Council of Ministers cannot seriously be likened to an upper chamber. It has no direct democratic legitimacy derived from the electors, but is in fact an inter-governmental body, and national parliaments have no control over commitments which the ministers from their countries undertake.The second possible role for a parliament is to make and unmake governments. In those system where this is the case, the parliament is the link between the preferences of the voters and the choice of a government.

The European Parliament's dilemma - its tragedy, even - is that it has no government to make or unmake. Worse, it does not even have a real say in the choice of the Commission. The Parliament has pressed to have a say in appointing the Commission President, be it only to have the theoretical right of rejection, and this was finally conceded in the Maastricht Treaty.Strictly according to the letter of the Treaty, the Parliament can censure the Commission - but know that were it to do so, the same body would continue in office with a care-taker mandate, and it would be the ministers, not the Parliament, that chose a new team - with the strong possibility that it might outface the Parliament by retaining the same...

This situation is absolutely central to the credibility of the Community system, and more particularly of the European elections, with the citizens of the Community. Elections, and the changes which they result in, are the moment that give voters in a parliamentary democracy the feel that they can influence events. If enough of them vote against the parties in government, and for other parties, then the composition of the government changes. With the steady personalisation of politics, it means that the voter can help determine who forms the next government - Kohl, or John Smith, or Edouard Balladur. Elections to the European Parliament totally lack this dimension.Whatever the result, whoever is President before the elections remains President after them.

The third possible role for a body elected by universal suffrage is that of "constituent assembly".This could become topical with the growing pressure for drawing up and adopting a European Constitution. In theory, the Parliament could, on the basis of the direct elections, claim to be a legitimate expression of the will of the peoples of the Community. But in practice, this could only occur if the Parliament - or an over-riding majority of its members - were prepared to challenge the member States head on, to make their claim to a constituent role their primary concern and the clash with the States a formal, public conflict. That such an approach is not possible reflects the realities of the situation: the governments are not prepared recognise any role of this kind for the European Parliament

The "D'Angelo-Santi clause" is a good illustration of this. D'Angelo-Santi was an Italian MEP, member of the Communist group, a lawyer by profession and a specialist in parliamentary procedure. He was struck by the fact that when the Parliament voted for changes in a Commission proposal, the Commission was in no way bound to take them into account. On his initiative, the Parliament altered its Standing Orders, so that if the Commission did not accept the most important amendments, the Parliament could refuse to adopt its opinion, and send the text back to committee. This obliged the Commission to take the Parliament more seriously. The idea was later taken over and further developed in the Single Act reforms, so that the Parliament now actually votes amendments to the legal texts submitted by the Commission, and can withhold them, thus halting the procedure, if the Commission will not formally accept them.

Opening up the Parliament

It would be a mistake to look at the Parliament purely in formal, institutional terms. A situation where formal political institutions are flawed may have a considerable potential impact in "civil society" terms. During the lifetime of the second European Parliament the "Green Alternative European Link - GRAEL", which was one component of the broader Rainbow Group, set out from the start to use this potential. A decision of principle was taken to attach as much importance to work for "the movement" outside the Parliament as to activities within it. Criteria for recruiting staff included movement experience, and the capability of organising an international conference. All political groups in the Parliament have the right to meeting rooms, with interpretation, for five days in each month. When the Group had met to discuss its parliamentary activities and internal affairs, there remained two days over, and these were used systematically for meetings organised with and for one or other movement organisation or to bring together others who as yet had no European-level network. In practice, owing to the dual pressure of European Parliament commitments and national politics, the Members of the Parliament in the GRAEL group often did little more than bless the meetings with their presence (to give them the status of "group meetings"), the rest was left to the respective members of the GRAEL team.

In this way, GRAEL assisted the Community-wide network of small

110

farmers' organisations that was challenging the impact of the Common Agricultural Policy. It brought together young people from all over Europe around the theme of "Youth and Racism" - and out of this grew a network of gay and lesbian organisations, with their own Europe resource unit. Lawyers met at GRAEL's invitation to compare experiences and plan cooperation in response to the plans for a European judicial area that would undermine the right of political asylum. One meeting in the series brought together those involved with workers' participation and self-management, twenty years on from 1968; and another, on the idea of a guaranteed minimum income, contributed to the establishment of an on-going independent network on that theme. GRAEL made the meeting facilities available for the second World Conference of Prostitutes, which after initial shock and surprise brought home to MEP's and press the seriousness of problems about health, repression and civil rights for whores. Also in the series was a meeting on the follow-up one year after the Tchernobyl nuclear disaster.

In some cases MEPs from the GRAEL were able to use the contacts and information emerging from these meetings in their work inside the Parliament. Paragraphs on the rights and working conditions of prostitutes were written into a major resolution adopted by the Parliament on women's rights generally. But it was the direct assistance and stimulus to Europe-wide "civil society" networking that was the more important. Unfortunately, the Green Alternative Link was the only political group to take this option, with the others continuing to use their meeting facilities only for preparing the work of the Parliament, or at the most for meetings of their own political family - and in doing so increasing the remoteness of their MEPs, and their parties, from a whole range of "civil society" concerns.The Single Act has overloaded the Parliament's already cumbersome machinery, with texts at every stage having to be provided in English, French, German, Italian, Spanish, Dutch, Danish, Greek and Portuguese..: now there is a flow of highly technical "legislation", understood by just a few specialists in a particular parliamentary committee, but having to go through first and second readings in committee and in plenary. When such texts appear in plenary, it is the same experts who speak, to a virtually empty chamber, and members vote as the experts of their group tell them to. At the same time, the Parliament does its best to act as a political body, debating all major political issues - but in doing so pays the price of demonstrating that it has virtually no influence on what the foreign ministers of the Twelve will decide, and still less on the "summit" meetings of the heads of government will decide.

There remains what may seem a minor, technical problem : the issue of the seat of Parliament. The European Parliament seems so remote, to most citizens of the member countries, that whether it meets in Strasbourg, Luxembourg or Brussels is hardly relevant. Yet in fact it holds the key to a lot of problems.The way the Parliament's work is currently organised is so patently inefficient and ineffective that it is hard at first to see why the Parliament tolerates it a day longer. The Parliament meets once a month in Strasbourg - from Monday at 5 pm to Friday at the end of the morning, with one night session. For this it has a hemicycle: but because that is also used, three times a year, for a week, by the Consultative Assembly of the Council of Europe, with its Europe-wide membership now beginning to include eastern European countries, the French authorities have decided to build a new hemicycle... It also has a building with an office-cum-bedsitter for each member, meeting rooms for political groups and for committees, and offices for almost its entire staff.For two other weeks of each month the parliamentary committees meet in Brussels, mostly for an afternoon and the following morning, so that Members arrive one day and depart the next. Active Members may well come one week for one committee, of which they are a full member, and the other week for another, in which they are alternate members (in practice no different from full membership). In Brussels, each Member has a second office; most of the staff of political groups are based there, with their offices, and so are some Parliament staff.

In the remaining week between plenary sessions, the political groups come together - sometimes in Brussels, but often making use of their right to meet in any Community capital, and once a year at a place of their choosing anywhere at all in the Community.What all this means to an active and conscientious Member is beyond belief. She or he must have a national base - which in the case of countries with a constituency system means a local office, able to cope with a never-ending (and ever-expanding) flood of demands for action, interest or information. To be effective,the Member also needs a base in Brussels, to keep up with what is going on in areas she or he is specialised in. Then there is the need for help during the non-stop activities of the plenary week in Strasbourg -which means in practice bringing someone in for a week from Brussels.

It is not only conflicting demands that pose a problem - the difficulty of working with three or more offices; it is not just the physical stress of continually shuttling from Strasbourg, to Brussels, to her/his national capital and to committee and group meetings all over Europe. That is how the problem hits the individual member. But the institution suffers too. Any parliament depends for its smooth running on a complex network of individual contacts, in and around the parliament itself and also with government departments. But the members of the EP have limited chances to get to know each other, or to work together. In Strasbourg there is an unrelenting pressure to attend informal meetings. In Brussels, in-and-out meetings make the chance of over-lapping with other members and having time to talk to them slight. A good member also needs time to develop contacts in the Commission and the complex world of lobbyists and experts, all centred in Brussels.

The whole system might indeed have been planned to ensure that it took the longest time possible for networks and caucuses to develop, across language barriers, and to make it as hard as possible for the Parliament to develop a sense of identity in relation to the other institutions. The mass of pressures to which Members are subjected, from local, national and European levels, and the total fragmentation of their lives, are hardly conducive to going deeply into issues or thinking and acting about fundamental challenges like the real status and powers of the Parliament.

The obvious answer to this messy situation is for the Parliament to have a single seat; and almost as obvious is that it should be Brussels. It is not only individual members that suffer from the fact that the Parliament currently falls between three stools - or three "seats". The institution as a whole packs less punch vis-a-vis both the Commission - where despite the lip service paid by the Commission in official statements, civil servants at all levels tend to treat the Parliament as a nuisance, making their lives more complicated - and the Council, which as far as it can ignores the Parliament and its views.

The situation is summed up in what happens to Commission proposals for Community " legislation". Formally, under the terms of the Treaties, the Council sends such texts to the Parliament for its opinion and for possible amendment. Only when it gets the text back - after first reading if it falls under the Single Act - with whichever amendments the Commission has agreed to, is the Council supposed to start examining it. What occurs in practice is that as soon as the Council receives the Commission's proposals, working parties of national experts start in on them. This is the start of the process that will lead eventually to the Council's decision, and all the way along, the Commission will amend its text to take account of compromises reached among the Twelve. Unfortunately for the Parliament, it works at another rhythm, and it will take anything from 4 to 8 months, depending on the importance of the text, for it go get through a procedure that involves appointment of a draftsperson, a first exchange in committee, an initial draft of amendments and resolutions, the opinions of other related committees, inclusion in the agenda of the plenary, and a debate and final vote. At the final stage, the Commission will be formally asked by the draftsperson, on behalf of the Parliament, whether it accepts the Parliament's amendments. By then, in all likelihood, the Council will be working on the basis of text many times revised, and departing widely from the draft on which the Parliament has been working. This the Commission cannot officially admit: but nor can it accept amendments from the Parliament which it knows already to have no chance of being accepted by the Council. The Parliament could in theory take the Council to the Court of Justice every time this occurred, but that would hardly increase its grip on the situation. The tough line would be to refuse to deal with Commission proposals when the examination in the Council was known to have begun. But that would call for the kind of aggressive assertion of its rights which, as we have seen, the Parliament is not prepared for.

9 Maastricht revisited

The Treaty of Maastricht was intended to mark a historic leap forward on the way to European unity. It has turned out to be more use as a barometer of the state of the Community, a measure of how little drive, idealism or unity of purpose there remains as regards the future of the integration process, yet at the same time the resilience of the institutional structures when faced with attacks from the inter-governmental camp.

The Maastricht operation has to be seen in the broader context of the attempt to revive that process, which began in the mid-'80s and is due to reach its climax in 1996. Besides a statutory revision of the Maastricht Treaty, there seems almost certain to be an effort to draw up Constitution for Europe. The assumption is also that by then a number of new countries will have become members, and contributing their input.

In the late '70s and early '80's the Community was stagnating. The introduction of direct elections to the European Parliament had failed to give it new dynamism, but it was pressing for some form of progress. The governments needed to have something to show for their European involvement, which was increasingly seen by public opinion as costly and bureaucratic. But the dual initiative to revive the Community came from two contrasting directions: from Jacques Delors, the newly appointed President of the Commission, and from the top bosses of Europe's biggest companies. Jacques Delors had been minister of finance in France in 1981-3, when outside pressures forced Mitterrand to abandon the Socialists' radical but inflationary economic programme, and opt for stability. Before that he had been chair of the European Parliament's committee on economic and monetary policy. Ambitious for himself and for the Community he was determined to re-launch the integration process. In his traditional round of visits to the heads of government of the Twelve, before taking office, he

115

offered them a choice of policies for revival: monetary union, institutional development; or cooperation on defence. But for each of these there was one prime minister at least who was against.

Delors then decided to fall back on the only topic that had aroused no opposition, probably because it seemed not to challenge national sovereignty, and was presented as a recipe for boosting growth and creating jobs. This "new" goal was the completion of a "common market" between the member countries - which was exactly the target originally set by the Rome Treaty, to be achieved over 12 years ending in 1970. The first steps - eliminating customs duties and quota restrictions, had been achieved, even ahead of time, because the business world was happy with the opening up of markets. But most of the other measures - free movement of capital, access to state procurement contracts in other member countries (from telephone exchanges to locomotives) had been blocked by vested interests in the member states. Now, a quarter of a century later, Delors was to have another try.

But this time, instead of meeting with reticence, the "single market" was welcomed. Big industry was behind it. Just as Delors was seeking his theme for revival, an informal club of the top managers from Europe's biggest firms (Philips, FIAT, Renault, but also Volvo - a dozen in all) had come to the conclusion that to hold their own in the face of the increasingly tough competition on world markets, they needed the biggest possible "home" markets. They would put their weight behind moves to eliminate all the economic frontiers that remained between one Community country and another. The example given by Philips, of needing 16 designs of electric plug to meet demand inside Europe, whereas only one was needed in the US or in Japan, told the story in a nutshell. Delors was certainly aware of these discussions, just as the industrialists were closely following Delors as he prepared to launch his initiative. Their backing was also a guarantee that the necessary Treaty would be accepted by the governments without difficulty: the Treaty was negotiated in 1986 and came into effect in 1988. It was known, oddly, as the "Single Act"- not because the governments wanted to do nothing else, but because a series of changes in the Community were all bundled together in a single document.

In the run-up to the preparations for the new Treaty, the Commission had called on outside consultants to carry out a massive study on what was called, equally oddly, "the cost of non-Europe", showing the disadvantage to businesses from the mass of persisting barriers. Delors seized on this, and presented it as evidence that the single market would mean a boost to growth and to employment - a claim of dubious worth, since figures in the report itself showed that many firms working for the public sector would not survive when subjected to competition, and that for two years at least the competitive jolt would mean a loss of jobs. But for Delors, the new style "common market" was just pump-priming. He was convinced that there would be a chain effect: with the removal of limitations on the movement of capital, fixed exchange rates would be needed, to avoid harmful uncertainty; but holding to fixed exchange rates would require a European central bank. At that point, it would be possible to introduce a single currency. Things went faster in that direction than had been expected. At the regular summit meeting of December 1989 a mandate was given for an Intergovernmental Conference to draw up a draft Treaty on Economic and Monetary Union. The project had the backing of the Committee of central bank governors, and was not opposed in meetings of the Council of ministers of economics. There was far-reaching consensus not only on the need for "EMU" but also on how it would be achieved.

What had not been thought through, and was certainly not the result of a consensus, was the decision to launch a parallel exercise to produce a draft for a Political Union. The initiative for this came above all from Germany. It was the German government that insisted that there had to be effective democratic control over monetary and economic policy. Pressure for this came from the German federal bank (Bundesbank) itself. Since it was common knowledge that a European Central Bank was going to be modelled on the Bundesbank, the other member countries could only follow the German recommendation. And the Treaty as drafted did indeed spell out the role of both the European Council (the summit) and the Council of Ministers for monetary and economic affairs, in supervising economic policy.

As for making the Community more democratic ("ending the democratic deficit" in Euro-jargon), all that the negotiators came up with was a procedure for to-ing and fro-ing between the European Parliament and the Council that filled a page and a half of Treaty, was totally intelligible even to experts, let alone the ordinary citizen, and resulted merely in giving the Parliament a veto right on a measure where the Council refused to compromise. The Parliament was quick to announce that it would avoid using the new procedure if at all possible.The way the rest of the Treaty on Political Union was drawn up was flawed in many ways. On the one hand, there was no consensus among the Twelve on what it was they wanted to do. What happened was the converse of the way the Community had acted in the past when progress was needed on a major issue: if there was not a consensus in favour, the idea would be dropped until it was ripe for decision.

117

But the Intergovernmental conference collected the things that various countries wanted to see enacted, and made them into a political package, which all had to accept if there was to be a Treaty at all. There was no minister or head of government with the wisdom or authority to say: halt! But the package did not represent a consensus on what they all of them actively wanted. So the Maastricht Treaty is a text that on paper does indeed seem to be most historic move ever made in the process of unification. The Twelve agreed to a single currency, a central bank, a common foreign policy, and a common defence policy. These are the policy areas that distinguish a nation state. Or, to put it another way: if a group of countries agree to act together, or to pool their sovereignty, on those matters, then they have effectively formed a federation.

Yet when the Maastricht Treaty was initialled, there was none of the jubilation, none of the talk about historic agreements, which this extraordinary document would seem to have merited. Instead, all attention was centred on the struggles that had marked the preparatory work, and the claims and counter-claims about who had "won". It was John Major, the United Kingdom prime minister, who went the furthest along this road. The UK stance throughout was confrontational: the negotiations at every level including heads of government were presented in "us"-versus-"them" terms; eliminating all reference to federalism was a success; and his refusal to agree to the Social Charter, which would be applied by the other Eleven, was a "victory" for the UK. In fact, on all the main policy areas except economic and monetary policy, the Treaty was like a city built on a seismic fault. The long-standing test of strength between those favouring the Community method and those preferring an inter-governmental approach had come to the surface, and been the object of Byzantine discussions. Delors, the Germans, and the Dutch (who were in the chair in the second half of 1991) insisted the Community should be seen as a tree, with the Community institutions developing naturally to cover new areas (foreign policy, defence...). Others, led by the British, peddled the idea of a "three pillars" construction. One pillar was the Community (which retains the name) including the machinery of the new economic and monetary union;an increase in the Community's powers in the fields of social and environmental policy, and an extension of its mandate to the areas of education and health. The second pillar covered foreign policy and defence, intended to remain the prerogative of the Council and the heads of government, but with a role carved out for Western European Union. The third pillar was "justice and home affairs", to be handled on a purely inter-governmental basis.This was what the negotiators had (inadvertently ?) called Chapter "K", dealing with right of asylum, immigration, police cooperation, and concerted action about drug trading and international crime.

Above the three was the European Council, giving the whole undertaking (now to be called the "Union" rather than the "Community") its priorities and its marching orders. But a close-up examination of the texts reveals the Commission popping up everywhere, like weeds, in the inter-governmental garden. Indeed, it is laid down from the start that the "Union" will use the institutional framework of the Community.

In the defence area, the Maastricht Treaty amounted to a sudden and unexpected lurch forward. Western European Union (a body hitherto largely moribund, and of which not all EC countries are members) was given a mandate to prepare proposals for the "Union" about defence issues, and to carry them out once they were approved. A special protocol gave a heavy-footed hint to the three EC countries not in WEU (Denmark, Greece and Ireland) that they should at least become observers, and in the long-run members. But the defence clauses built into the heart of the Treaty another long-standing tension: between the British,Dutch and Portuguese, determined that the Community should develop as a "European pillar of NATO", and the French in particular (backed by the Spanish and Germans) who saw slipping Western European Union into the Maastricht Treaty with a key role as a way of affirming a European identity in the defence field.

The idea of a common foreign policy was an area where there was no apparent disagreement. The Twelve had been only too aware of their incapacity to function as a unit in the face of major events like the UN-covered American war against Irak, or the break-up of the Yugoslavian federation.

But events subsequent to the initialling of the Maastricht Treaty drove home the hard fact that a common foreign policy, let alone any kind of joint military initiative, be it for peace-keeping, cannot be brought into being over-night. The regular consultations among the foreign ministers of the Twelve over recent years had not prepared them for joint action. The procedures written into the Maastricht Treaty, with provision for deciding unanimously where majority voting should apply, pre-supposed a readiness to make compromises, in order to achieve agreement on joint action, which simply did not yet exist. Had the Twelve been ready to act together, the delay over the ratification of the Treaty would not have mattered, and the procedure could have been used de facto whilst awaiting the coming into force of the Treaty. But the Community found itself unprepared to react as a unit to the foreign policy options forced on it from every side: the Yugoslavian crisis; US chest-thumping about Irak and its nuclear installations (where the French and British were just as prepared to act as US lackeys as they had been in the original war); the Somalian tragedy (where the Community waited until the United States took the initiative); the new American aggressivity over international trade; and the appeals from the central and eastern European countries for gestures of political solidarity as future EC partners (though here at least the Commission did take the initiative).

The notion of Maastricht as being in some ways a dress rehearsal for a more successful move towards unification is not far from the truth. Reactions to the Treaty - both to the way it was drawn up, behind closed doors, and to its far-reaching content - had a profound impact. The "NO" in the Danish referendum, the vote in the French referendum, won by the smallest of margins, and the warning noises about sovereignty from the German Constitutional Court, were so many clear signals that any grandiose plans for the future would have to be subject to far-reaching public debate. When it comes to 1996, very probably with the drafting of a Constitution, the facts will show whether the lessons of Maastricht have been learned.

10 Towards utopia

To react to the inter-locking crises that loom over human society and over the planet is going to require radical changes in accepted values and dominating behaviour. An economic system destructive of human dignity and of the planetary environment, and the resulting decline in the credibility of democracy: these are the underlying crises to which the answers currently on offer are disappointing and inadequate.

The questions this text seeks to answer concern the role of the Europeans, and of whatever policy-making institutions they may succeed in establishing. Will they, with the same narrowness of vision that have marked - and marred - the last four decades, continue to sustain the prevailing economic system, which as we can more and more clearly see, is responsible for much of the destruction ? Or will they prove able to draw on their resources - democratic traditions, constitutional experience, economic might and technical skills - to take the lead in developing a non-destructive world society, based on economic and ecological solidarity ?

Changes of the kind that will be needed - replacement of a prevailing system of political economy by a system with other values and priorities - have tended in the past to take place imperceptibly, usually under the pressure of technical and economic developments, without conscious policy-making. But in the unprecedented struggle that is now joined, pitting the high priests and the lackeys of the prevailing system of production-and-destruction against the prophets of solidarity and a non-destructive economy, with the planet as backdrop, there is no way of knowing who is winning. We cannot afford, in the terms of Lester Brown's water-lily parable, just to wait and see when the lilies will fill the pond. For what is at stake, in a new approach to the economy, to the environment and to peace, is no less than survival.

At present, it is at the European level that there are the best chances of this

121

challenge being taken up - despite the Europeans' resounding failure so far in their efforts to unite.The very size and weight of the economic and political unit emerging in Europe gives it the potential to change the course of events. Also, the next few years are due to see the drafting and adoption of a Constitution for Europe. This will imply not only the development of viable federal institutions, but also a definition of Europe's goals and values, in organising its own society and in playing its role in the world.

To achieve lucid discussion of the options that lie ahead it is important to distinguish different modes, and different time-tables. One way to achieve a new approach to political economy is to elaborate a vision - better, perhaps, a utopia -which can serve as a point of reference and provide basic inspiration. The defenders of the prevailing economic system have no such vision around which to mobilise, no utopia to inspire them, other than the worn-out liturgies about "growth" and economic revival. Their system is destructive (not least of jobs) when it is working well, and more destructive when it is failing.

In the present world situation, resulting from the unpredictable events that led to the implosion of the communist régimes, the confrontation of two conflicting "models" has given way to a situation where on the face of it there is only one system on offer: the "free market" system, with its corollary, the permanent green light for unbridled competition. But to see the free market as a system without an opponent is misleading: a new dichotomy is emerging, between the system hitherto prevailing (which is now spreading to every corner of the planet), and an alternative whose philosophy is that of the "green left".

True, this alternative vision is still far from being widely known or accepted. Many of the strands from which it would have to be woven are present, in the work of researchers, in the programmers of progressive parties, in the rich and complex experience of local and regional government, and of civil society groups. But for lack of an organised institutional framework, it is hard to achieve a single, shared vision that can provide a starting-point for personal and political commitment.

The aim of the first part of this text has been to provide an overview of the context within which a vision of a new political economy would have to be worked out: the dimension of the crises, the record of the Europeans, and a possible constitutional framework. Against that background there are three distinct exercises that can be attempted. The first is the elaboration of the long-term political vision. The second concerns the drafting and adoption of the Constitution, the commitments that will be written into it, and the new life which it should bring to democratic processes in Europe and beyond: that is a matter for the coming months and years. The third is a matter of reflection on what could be the most difficult challenge of all : how to translate a growing public awareness and commitment into fundamental change in both institutions and policies. This is particularly crucial when the prevailing system, sensitive to any threat, can be expected to react with all the resources at its disposal, not least domination of the media.

Just as the crises and challenges of the fin du siècle spring from the destructive power of the prevailing economic system -undermining societies by plant closures, demoralising and humiliating people through unemployment, destroying the delicate balance of the eco-sphere - so solutions must involve a fundamental break with that system.

The values and attitudes which constitute the ground rules for the operation of the world economy amount to a right to take and a right to destroy. It is a sort of imperialism of the "haves" over the "have nots", a colonisation by man of the riches and beauty of the environment.

What is needed in its place is a new political economy, an economic and social system based on values and attitudes that can best be reserved in two words: solidarity and husbandry. Solidarity is evocative of a positive attitude of people above all to each other, but also to the eco-sphere and to generations to come. Husbandry, with its roots in the relations of the individual to the household and the land, is the most expressive term for a caring and responsible impact of mankind, with all its dangerous tools and techniques, on the ecology of the planet; and also for a concern to sustain customs and traditions - crafts, skills, accumulated wisdom about life in groups.

From the central notion of solidarity flows a commitment to a basic level of economic activity ensuring that the recognised individual needs (material but also social and cultural) of all who dwell on the planet are met; and that minimal levels of collective well-being are also guaranteed. But once that level is reached, the target is no longer to maximise but to minimise production.

From the equally central notion of husbandry flows, likewise, a commitment to individual and collective respect and care for the natural environment, of which mankind must act as a responsible, integrated and above all non-destructive part; and similar care for the heritage of accumulated institutional wisdom and cultural creativity.

The two notions solidarity and good husbandry are complementary and inter-twined. The goals for levels of individual and collective well-being must be tempered by the obligation to the environment; care for the environment is in its turn an expression of solidarity with future generations, for whose sake the destructive impact of economic activity must be eliminated.

A utopia is not a blue-print, still less is it a party programme, to be put into practice, pragmatically, upon coming to power. Rather is it the broad set of options, principles and commitments that provide long-term inspiration for political action.

Central to an alternative vision of the future is the position of the individual in the economic process : production, consumption, transport, waste - and in particular the position of work. At present, the economic process world-wide embodies uncritically the work ethic: work is the source of individual income, and trade unions and governments recognise a right to work. But technical developments have steadily reduced the amount of work needed to achieve the same result, at every stage of the production cycle. First came the replacement of physical work by machines. Now mental work (typing, accounting) is being rendered superfluous by other (technological) machines. Ahead lies the third stage when conceptual work (designing, programming, planning) can be carried out by computers.

Employers have welcomed this trend, which weakens the position of organised labour, and makes employers less dependent on workers, save in a few key positions for which the competition is savage. But the problem comes to roost with governments, committed to "creating jobs" in a context where "growth", to which they are also committed, involves reducing not increasing the amount of work.In this situation, many formulas are under discussion. Most of them stop short at the idea of work sharing.It is assumed that this can be achieved by reducing the working hours of some, in order to make work available for others. But it is a formula that runs into many difficulties. Thus employers do all they can to avoid creating new jobs which involve a range of social security commitments. Their preference is for "flexible contracts", under which workers can be laid off if there is a down-turn in the economy, or jobs are subject to a "last in, first out" clause which has the same effect. The basic snag is that if work-sharing does not reduce the wage bill, employers are not interested; and if it does reduce it, the workers are against. A fundamental social and political objection to work sharing is that it confirms the "two tier" approach resulting from unemployment -the discrimination between those with and those without a job. Finally, job sharing does nothing to halt (still less to reverse) the decline in the number of jobs.

124

A vision of a far more radical and coherent approach is possible. It would be based on breaking the link between work and income, and would involve three elements: first, a guaranteed basic income for all; second, an equal work obligation for all those able to work; and third, a shift from maximum production to minimum production as the underlying rule for the economy.

Maximising production is at the heart of the prevailing economic system. It is presented as contributing to a higher "standard of living", as reflected in a high level of consumption. In reality this means a maximalisation of the profits obtained at each stage of the production cycle. An increased level of production/consumption is also what is used to determine the "rate of growth" - for governments still make growth the yardstick of economic prosperity and successful management of the economy. But the present economic crisis - with unemployment at its core - stems precisely from the fact that almost all the activities falling under the heading of production involve a greater or lesser degree of destruction. So maximum production also implies a maximum of destruction.

Whence the need to switch from a system based on maximum production to one based on minimum production - at least until the link between production and destruction has been eliminated.

There are many ways in which the level of destruction, resulting from the various stages of the production process can be reduced to a minimum. One is the use of a maximum of recyclable materials - with the obligation that they be effectively re-cycled. Taking the example of drink containers, the initial production of the metal may involve damage to the natural environment where the ore is mined, and heavy energy consumption; but by re-cycling the metal the repetition of the whole destructive cycle can be limited.

A second strand in this approach is the use of a maximum of renewable energy. There is the potential to meet all energy demand from renewable sources, thus reducing damage done by other sources (hydrocarbons, nuclear power stations) to a minimum and finally fading them out.

A third factor is the switch from the current emphasis on throw-away consumer goods to long-life products. This, like the concept of a minimum level of production, runs contrary to the approach and the interests of the prevailing economic system, and can be sure to arouse hostility. The long-life product has several advantages: it reduces the demand for consumer goods, which do not need to be continually replaced; in so far as long-life products are crafted, they add to the amount of work (rewarding work) available.

The second reversal of direction, potentially forming part of a strategy for change, is the idea of a guaranteed minimum income. The basic idea, on which there are many variants, is that all citizens - not just workers or former workers, but the old, children, the handicapped - receive a uniform guaranteed income throughout their lives. This goes at least some of the way towards removing the stigma from unemployment. As generally conceived, this formula is intended to replace the various hand-outs (pensions, children's allowances, free health care) from which some benefit and not others. One of the open questions concerns the benefits (free schooling, free medical care) which might still be free or might have to be met from the basic income.

The complement to this initiative lies in a third principle, which also contributes to eliminating the link between work and income: the individual obligation to provide the collectivity with a given amount of work. The starting-point is again the fact that there is less work needed than the "working population" is able to supply. The answer often proposed, as already noted, is to cut working hours and leave it to the play of the free market to determine whether this is producing more employment. The French left-wing economist Andre Gore, and others who have taken up his ideas, have opted for a more visionary approach. The starting-point is the amount of working hours required to meet society's needs. This is divided by the number of workers, to yield the total amount of work required, in a working life-time, from all those able to work. A rough estimate is that this figure might, at present, amount to half the hours currently worked. Each worker would then be obliged, in her/his life-time, to work that amount of hours, but would be free as regards the pattern of time worked: it could be a full working week for half a working life-time, followed by early retirement; or half-time every day; or alternating working a year and travelling or studying for a year; or working in the winter and going south in the summer... The worker would thus be meeting an obligation to society, and free to shape her/his life instead of having the pattern of it imposed by work commitments. Naturally, there are many details that would have to be worked out: it is the stimulus to more radical thinking that is the most important if change is to be brought about.

There are many other paths that need to be followed up, in order to lay sound foundations for debate about an alternative political economy. Most of them, taken separately, will seem controversial to say the least. Taken as a whole, they are intended as a contribution to wide-ranging debate.

Consumption guidelines. A parallel approach, tending in the same direction as the notion of minimum production, has to do with admissible levels of consumption. This arises from the common - and wholly predictable - popular reaction to the idea of any restriction on consumption, such as is implied, for instance, by references to "zero growth". This problem was tackled head-on, in the 70's, by Aurelio Peccei, vice-president of FIAT, in the first Report to the Club of Rome, a group of industrialists concerned about ecological destruction. Peccei spelt out the implications of the exponential growth which was the chosen pattern of behaviour of the rich industrialised economies, and pointed out that if all citizens of the world were to follow the same path, the world would be destroyed long before they all reached western living standards. That was a quarter of a century ago; yet the underlying approach to growth remains unchanged.

Indeed, with those same living standards still upheld as the model to be attained, Peccei's problem remains intact.So why should not the statistical and computer technology skills now available be used to establish a body of knowledge about levels of sustainability. It would be the task of an independent body, under the auspices of the United Nations, to provide data about levels of consumption currently prevailing, and their implications in terms of consumption of non-renewable resources. It would also have the task of assessing what living standards could be generalised to the people of the planet within the context of a sustainable economy. The research would distinguish scenarios based on current patterns of resource use from others involving a maximum of re-cycling, renewable energy and materials, and long-life products.

Progress in acceptance of lower consumption targets could be furthered by a series of other moves. One would be the development of formulas for assessing citizens' well-being, taking into account income level, access to public services (training and education, health, information), ecological surroundings, cultural and other long-life possessions... This "quality of life index" would be drawn up, published and debated world-wide. It would necessarily not produce only comparisons of national averages, but take in major divergences between groups within countries. The aim of such an index would not be to provide a basis for action, but to provide the background for steady pressure for the elimination of the worst imbalances.

Democratic control. Vital to an alternative approach to the economy - but absent of course under the prevailing economic system - is democratic control. The kind of utopia outlined here could not function without effective limitations - democratically adopted and carried out - on concentrations of economic power: multinational banks and companies, industrial lobbies (oil, nuclear, chemicals...). Among the various possible approaches are : a guaranteed role for workers' organisations in the policy-making of multinational companies, on the basis of access to information; an international (UN backed) body to monitor the activities of multinational companies; close control, using the latest technology, over the activities of speculators... If these ideas indeed sound "utopian", then it is only because there has been no pressure to move in the direction of world-level control over forces working world-wide. That is due, once again, to the absence of institutions capable of channelling democratic pressures.

Trade: not too free. It has been part of the established wisdom of the prevailing economic system that free trade is sacred, and any departure from it constitutes a threat to world prosperity. "Protectionism" is the bogey word. But there is a growing realisation that GATT (the General Agreement on Tariffs and Trade), which is the world-level guardian of free trade, is in reality an instrument with which the rich countries exploit their poorer trading partners. In trade between rich and poor, it always the rich who come off best.International trade is an occasion for exploitation. It diverts resources from the poorer countries, where they are needed, via international banks and companies to the richer countries. Trade results in transport, which uses non-renewable energy sources and adds to pollution of the air (kerosene) and the seas (oil).An alternative world vision has as its target a minimum of trade. As far as possible, national economies are based on self-reliance. Needs that cannot be met from a country's own resources or skills can be obtained on the basis of bilateral or multi-lateral deals and trading relations.

Policies for peace. In a vision of a world at peace, the Europeans have a major role to play. One vital element is the phasing out of the arms trade, so that European economies no longer depend on the sale of lethal weaponry to ensure their trade balance. Second, Europe has to develop a force conceived and trained for peace-making and peace-keeping, both within Europe and under European command, and elsewhere in the world under United Nations command. There is no reason why all European countries, whatever their status in the Union, should take part in the European Peace Force. A minimal standing force is needed, ready for action, with contingents from many countries, but other countries might opt to participate on an ad hoc basis in European Union or United Nations activities.

Water: preventing conflict. Access to and sharing out of water supplies is certain to be a source of conflict all over the planet in the years ahead. It would be wise to act now, and establish a body with both the technical skills and the mediating experience to forestall the conflicts which otherwise threaten to occur. This could be done under the auspices of the United Nations. The initiative might be taken by the Europeans, as a gesture of their concern for world-level problems.

Soft energy. One aspect of the utopia towards which the Europeans will be striving concerns energy. The target is clear and simple: to build future European society purely on renewable energy sources, eliminating sources currently used (nuclear power, hydrocarbons) which are dangerous and non-renewable. Soft, renewable energy has a de-centralising effect on the economy, and is a source of employment in design, manufacture and maintenance.

Regional autonomy. An alternative political economy will leave more space for the autonomous development of regions. An adequate degree of political autonomy, combined with regional resources (material and human), offers a chance for regions to find their own responses to many of the key challenges. There is no need for a uniform pattern of regional development: on the contrary, disparate traditions and resources, complemented by a guarantee of political autonomy, can result in a mosaic of differing patterns. Economically powerful central regions will be developing, soaking up resources, and the gaps between them and outlying rural areas are likely to increase. But the alternative vision is one of solidarity, with a generous system of "perequation", transferring resources from the richer to the poorer areas.
In the kind of utopia of which this would be part, peripheral areas, with appeal in terms of environment, climate and quality of life, could exercise as much pull as over-crowded central areas with highly-developed economies and high levels of stress.

Self-management. Thinking about forms of self-management has tended to be relegated to the ideological back-burner, as left and progressive forces find themselves on the defensive against the onslaughts of privatisation and the dismantling of the welfare state. But self-management of work and at work is an inextricable element in the kind of utopia so briefly outlined here. It slots into a continuum with democratic control over powerful economic

129

forces, and with the development of autonomy at regional and perhaps lower levels.

Constitution for Europe

It has emerged repeatedly from the history of the attempts to unite Europe, that the main handicap was the lack of a viable institutional framework. It was this that prevented people from being presented with key policy choices. Now it would seem that the Europeans are set on giving themselves one last chance: the closing months of 1993, and early 1994, saw growing attention been given to the idea of a European Constitution, and a deadline - 1996 - looming, near enough to be taken seriously.

There have been indications of very different kinds, all pointing in roughly the same way. If some or all of the four candidates for full Community/Union membership do effectively join, then it may prove necessary to amend the functioning of the Community. At the formal level, the Maastricht Treaty comes up for revision in 1996. Politically, the governments of the member States were shaken by the negative popular reaction to Maastricht: the initial Danish "NO", the close-run French referendum, the hostility in the House of Commons, and perhaps most of all the cautious ruling of the German Constitutional Court. They are going to want to restore the appeal of the "European idea". That they can only hope to do if the negotiating process is transparent, and there is widespread consultation. Whether such a powerful dose of openness is one they are prepared to face, remains an open question. But there is undoubtedly a growing feeling that instead of tinkering with the Maastricht text (already unintelligible to the ordinary citizen) the Europeans should take the braver and more significant step of drawing up a Constitution. A third aspect of the situation is the inescapable responsibility of the leaders of western Europe towards their fellow Europeans. The Community has been providing by far the lion's share of financial support and technical assistance for the countries of central and eastern Europe, but has tended to shy away from commitments in the fields of foreign policy or security, for which the countries concerned had hoped. In drawing up a Constitution there would be no avoiding the need to define the status to which the various groups of countries could aspire: Hungary, Poland, Slovakia and the Czech Republic;Bulgaria and Romania; the three Baltic states (Estonia, Lattvia and Lithuania); Switzerland, if it does not opt for membership); Malta, Cyprus, Turkey...Politically, they would not be ushered into the political waiting room, while the EC/EU members drafted a Constitution for a European political unit to which they could then choose to adhere.

The European Parliament's committee on institutional affairs did not wait for the ratification of the Maastricht Treaty before starting work on drafting a Constitution for the newly fledged European Union. Unfortunately, what happened when it came up in plenary session went to show that the Parliament would probably not be the best body to pursue the issue: the main political parties decided not to vote on the substance of the proposals, but to welcome the report... and leave the proposals in an annex, neither accepted nor rejected.

Meanwhile, the idea of a Constitution began to spread. Significantly, it is favoured by the various federalist movements, but also by some "anti-Europeans", in particular in the United Kingdom Conservative Party, who see the Constitution as a chance to re-shape the Community along inter-governmental lines. That was an attempt made in the Maastricht negotiations; but the Treaty as it emerged confirmed the role of the Community institutions, and while some other countries may share UK reluctance about a federal structure for the Union, they will not take the path of dismantling what has been achieved over the past four decades.

The significance of drafting a Constitution will lie in its putting clearly the genuine "federal question": the choice between a Community system where decisions are taken by the representatives of the States (even if the Parliament is also involved), and a system where decisions are taken by an authority acting under a direct, democratic, federal mandate.

Given the virtually unlimited potential of an all-European grouping, the choices that lie before the European countries and their citizens merit a full, democratic debate. This must last the time that is needed (and certainly a matter of months and years), and involve a maximum of consultation of both established political organisations and citizens in their civil society movements.

The drafting and adoption of a Constitution could be a democratic process totally without precedent in European history. The failure of such a attempt would be equally momentous.

It does not fall within the scope of this essay to speculate about the likely options that may emerge, or the final outcome. A few preliminary points may however be worth making.

 - Who calls for the Constitution ?   - not just the politicians, but a broad movement of citizens ?

- Who convenes the drafting process ? - is it the heads of government, or the parliaments ?
- Who does the drafting ? - what stages are behind closed doors, and when is there open consultation and debate ?
- What provision is made for popular consultation ? - will there be national referendums ? or a Europe-wide referendum ?
- What will be the roles of the European and national parliaments in ratification ?
- What will be the required majority ? - for instance, what combination of referendum and ratification results, in what proportion of the countries...
This gives some indication of the complexity of the process, and the seriousness with which it will need to be prepared.
Inevitably, in the process planned for 1996, there will not only be talk of the institutional side of the drafting process, but debate on what areas of policy the Constitution should cover e.g. what broad goals will be written in, in the areas of economic rights, of human rights and civil liberties, of peace policy, of commitments about solidarity with the third world.
So a decision to go ahead with drafting a Constitution will be the starting-point for a broad political debate that is long overdue - which may be why the party organisations in the European Parliament preferred to postpone, until after the up-coming European Parliament elections, the debate on even the anodyne and far from visionary text adopted at the Committee stage...

Thoughts on transition

Far and away the biggest challenge to developing a new political economy is the problem of transition, in the face of resistance that can be expected to range from hostility to sabotage, from ridicule to censorship. Supposing that a broad and coherent vision of the future has begun to mature, and take its place in people's minds - a utopia from which inspiration can be drawn... Assuming, then, that a growing proportion of the population are becoming aware of the alternative, and are attracted and perhaps even convinced by it... What are the chances of moving from this situation to one where real changes are made, perhaps even inroads into the prevailing system. The issue of this transition period could well turn out to be the key to the success or failure of alternative policies in the coming years.
Clearly, the process is more arduous than its equivalent within the framework of one country. Where there is an established democratic system,

ideas can be tested in elections at different levels. At the Europe-wide level, as has transpired time and again in this analysis, the appropriate institutions are lacking. Above all, there is no executive body with a democratic mandate, under democratic control.

It is also true that our society is not kind to visions, or to visionaries. In the past, it was by a steady and determined process of persuasion and assimilation that people, and ideas, won ascendancy. Today, the visionary is condemned to run the gauntlet of the media - above all television. She or he will be picked up and shaken, until all their ideas fall out, with as much information as possible about their personal and private lives falling out as well. After a while - longer or shorter, it changes little - the editors will judge that the visionary is no longer attracting an audience, and she/he will sink without trace. And because the media home in on individuals, rather than ideas, once the visionary has gone, the vision is unlikely to survive.

But there are also more fundamental arguments. There are those - pessimists ? realists? - who are convinced that the prevailing economic system is too deeply-rooted for any real change to be achieved. Clearly, the prevailing forces will be aware of the kind of utopia which is being developed as an alternative to their system. There will be holds barred in the struggle, the main battlefield for which will be the media. The utopia will be attacked head-on, as being "unrealistic" and unworkable, and ideas for the long term dismissed as though they were proposals for radical change overnight. The favourite target will be any aspect of the long-term vision, any of the measures in an alternative political programme, that can be presented as a threat to levels of individual income.

The pattern of alternating stagnation and change, that has marked the attempts at unification over the past four decades, seems to point to two basic conditions that have to be met, if there is going to be a chance of replacing the prevailing economic system. One is an alliance between the forces primarily concerned about work, and those primarily concerned about ecological issues. This is the red-green (or green left) alliance that has been attempted in some countries, but has rarely been based on a coherent approach combining the two concerns. Nor is it easy, for trade unions fighting a losing battle on the central issue of jobs, to take on board the radical notions - such as minimum production - which point the way to a coherent analysis but are far distant from traditional trade union problems.

The other condition is the alliance of political parties from the green-left spectrum with "civil society" groups and movements. This offers the best prospect of a two-pronged pressure: the gradual, but never measurable, spread of awareness and concern about environmental issues; and the pressure of public opinion, which has the potential to affect parties on a far broader spectrum (witness the pressure for a tax on fuels contributing to the green house affect). By their very nature, unions, parties and groups are unlikely to lend themselves to any attempt at a broad front departing from the traditional political dividing lines. On the other hand, there is probably more scope than has hitherto been realised on either side for ad hoc alliances and action on specific issues. (One of the issues which would lend itself the best to such an ad hoc approach would be arms industry conversion, in conjunction with an on-going pressure for disarmament.The challenge would be to carry out the re-training of skilled workers from the arms industries. The target would be to enable them to design and teach appropriate methods for producing anti-pollution or alternative energy technologies.).

The media, with their immense capacity for persuasion, and with the prospect of techniques making their message all-pervading, will be at the centre of the struggle for radical change, being at once the object and the instrument of the encounter. The key may well lie both in techniques of resistance to media impact - a sort of induced immunity, based on new work and living relationships, and in skills in the use of the media to induce a parallel immunity to the domination of the consumerised economy. In both cases, the answer will lie in refusing passivity and nurturing a deep-rooted attachment to both solidarity and independence. That is one at least of the possible keys to survival, both of a society to live in and a planet surviving.

Whale epilogue

The story of what mankind has done to whales is a parable for the wider record of what we have done, and are doing, to the natural world. Most human civilisations have treated nature as though it were there for their use, not to respect and wonder at - still less to cherish as something of which human beings are a part. The current system, industrial and materialist, is the most threatening by far. It is establishing its domination in every last corner of the planet, and in so doing is exterminating not only other species but groups of human beings who had hitherto sustained a different way of life, with other values. As usual with humanity's greatest crimes, the periodic flare-ups of human genocide and the extermination of whole species, the extent of the massacre has been minimised, and its impact kept as secret as possible. The breakthrough to the mass killings of whales came with the invention of the harpoon gun and the explosive harpoon head, precursor of - and as cruel as - shrapnel bomb later invented for human targets. What had been a dangerous profession, which took its toll in human lives, became an unending massacre.

In the struggle that has taken place since World War II, in and around the International Whaling Commission, whales were talked about as though they were just another, rather bigger, form of fish, to be "harvested" as long as stocks permitted. Thus as each species of whale was decimated, and its survival became problematical (and, of course, hunting it had ceased to be profitable...), it would be put on the list of protected species. Public opinion was concerned about preventing the sheer cruelty of the killing; government representatives could only be reasoned with in terms of the threatened extinction - of species they had written off.

But the qualitative arguments are the most telling. Research has demonstrated that whales and other sea mammals have an intelligence (as

135

measured by the dimensions of the cerebral cortex) comparable to and in some cases outstripping that of human beings. This also applies - as is being realised far too late - to elephants, another species with intelligence comparable to that of mankind, for which extinction threatens. Simple observation over centuries has shown, without a shadow of doubt, that sea mammals behave in ways that humans have always seen as marking them off from all other species. They sing (complex songs, transmitted from year to year), play games (involving large groups), and make love. All these activities take more time in their lives than seeking nourishment. They show solidarity in misfortune (whales supporting a wounded comrade); and in certain cases revenge for harm done to them. Despite the record of our inhumanity in whale hunting, there are many substantiated stories of whales guiding to safety vessels which were lost in fog or among the ice.

In the context of mankind's restless and pretentious quest to understand not just the bio-sphere but the rest of the universe, to achieve communication with whales and dolphins is surely as great an intellectual challenge as any on the planet. To suggest this, after the bloodbath of several hundred years, is presumptuous in the extreme. It will have to be done in a spirit of reconciliation - and not with the same mentality that has trained dolphins to carry bombs in man's inter-tribal warfare.

Whereas whales, because of their size, remained distant and mysterious, there have always been close relations between dolphins and humans. It is tragic that just as the end of whale hunting may be in sight, there is a new massacre under way: that of the dolphins.It is taking place mainly as a non-caring side-effect of tuna-fishing.

Few people stop to ask themselves for what all the dead whales of the decades of massacre were needed. Heathcote Williams,in his epic poem in honour of the "Whale Nation", spells out to what an extent our comfortable and complex industrial society was built on products of the whale - above all sperm oil (first for candles, more recently for lubricants for space trave)l. He shows that most of the coastal cities in the northern hemisphere grew prosperous from industries that depended on whaling. If the halting of whaling had been called for in the last century, it would have met with the cry "We cannot do without it..".Today, however, there is not a single product of whale killing that cannot be produced with other, artificial materials. Even the special lubricants can be extracted from the jojoba plant, which can be used to win back land from the deserts.

The campaign against whale killing is an example of the pattern that repeats itself regularly with efforts to end particular cases of irreversible

136

ecological destruction. First came the commitment of a few individuals - in this case David McTaggart and his Greenpeace crew, on its way back from direct action against French nuclear testing in the Pacific. Then the cause was taken up by a growing circle of others, and began to find its echo in the media. That was the start of the long struggle to win over opinion, and then to put the relevant authorities under pressure until they acted. Then there was (indeed still is) another cause for concern: how to bring to an end an activity formally outlawed but continuing in practice.

Finally, there is the most exciting phase of all: the challenge to enter into communication with whales and dolphins. But in the meantime, the story of the attempt to the save the whales raises the same issues as the broader struggle over the future of the planet. The moratorium has a good chance of becoming permanent, and if so, the whales need no longer fear the harpoons and the factory ships. Their image of mankind will be modelled, instead, on the growing numbers of eco-tourists who pay to see them at close quarters, free in their natural habitat.

But there is one last twist to the tale, perhaps the saddest part of all. The whales' universe, the high seas in which they can communicate with each other round half the globe, and migrate from one ocean to another, are being increasingly over-run by the noise of ships (hard to bear for the whales' sensitive sonar systems), and poisoned by oil and other waste. We can only speculate as to whether the groups of whales which strand themselves, and refuse rescue, are in fact committing a form of collective suicide rather than face the deterioration of their world, and the suffering which it brings. So we face another of these disturbing situations, where there are competing negative and positive trends. Out of a world of natural beauty, humankind has conjured up polluted, over-crowded cities, fraught with illness and violence. Have we saved the whales from the harpoon, merely to render their natural environment unlivable ?

If the whales should die out, it will spell the end of life on the planet.This is in part for a practical reason: the death of the whales could shatter be yond repair the balance of the food chain of which the plankton-eating baleen whales are the crucial link. But it is also for a reason that is political: if mankind, with its knowledge and resources, has failed to save the whales, from its own voracity and its own destructive materialistic economy, then what hope can there be for living in harmony as part of planet earth...

Bibliography

Note about the bibliography. There is an immense and steadily increasing volume of academic material about all aspects of the European Community. It is overwhelmingly uncritical in its approach. As a journalist rather than an academic, the author has relied on the publications of the Community's own institutions (essentially the Commission and the Parliament), on the day-to-day flow of specialised reporting which is available, and not least on long years of critical discussion about what the integration process means and where it is headed.

agenor (1975-1993) Series of pamphlets (Nos 51-111) covering developments in the European Community and social movements. agenor, Brussels.
"Agence EUROPE", Brussels.(Daily newsletter on the European Community and the whole gamut of "European" activities, published in Brussels, and providing a reliable information base for all those involved in the integration process).

Bonde, J.-P.(1993), *Unionen efter Maastricht & Edinburg (The Union after Maastricht and Edinburgh)*, Notat, Denmark (in Danish).
Brown, L.R.(1978) *The Twenty-Ninth Day*, Worldwatch Institute, Norton, New York;
Brown, L.R.(1981), *Building a Sustainable Society*, Worldwatch Institute, New York
Brown, L.R., et.al.(1991), *State of the World*, Worldwatch Institute, Norton, New York
Brundtland,G.H., and World Commission on Environment and Development, (1987), *Our Common Future*, OUI.
Bunyan,T., (1993), *Statewatching the new Europe*, Statewatch, London.

Conroy, C. and Litvinoff, M., Ed.(1988), *The Greening of Aid*, Earthscan
Publications Ltd., London.'
Le dossier Creys-Malville (The Creys-Malville file)(1990), Editions Slatkine,
Geneve
Day,D.,(1992), *The Whale War*, Grafton, London
Fuchs.J. and Schuster J.,Ed.(1993), *Zwischen Nationalstaat und
Globalpolitik (Between the Nation State and Global Policy)*, spw-Verlag
(in German).
GRIP,(1992),*Les Conflits Verts (The Green Conflicts)*, Brussels.
George, S.(1988), *A Fate Worse Than Debt*, Pelican, London
Groen, M. and van Brakel, M.(1987), *De Aarde Verliest Grond (The World
is Losing Ground)*, Jan van Arkel, Utrecht (in Dutch).
Harrison, P., (1992-93), *The Third Revolution*, Penguin, London
Katholische Sozialakademie Osterreichs (Austrian Social Academy), (1977),
Heraus aus der Krise - wohin? (Out of the Crisis - where to?)
Lovelock, J. (1988),*The Ages of Gaia*, Oxford University
Monnet J., (1976), *Mémoires*, Fayard, Paris (in French)
Olivi, B. and Ducci, A. (1970), *L'Europa Incompiuta (Unfinished Europe)*,
Cedam, Padova. (Documents in Eng., Fr.,It.)
Olivi,B., (1994), *L'Europa Politica (Political Europe)*, Cedam,
(Documents in Eng.,Fr.,It.)
Postel,S.,(1992), *Last Oasis: facing water scarcity*, Norton, New York,
Raikes,P.(1988), *Modernising Hunger*, Catholic Institute for International
Relations, London
Scheer,H.,(1986), *Die Befreiung von der Bombe' (Freed from the Bomb)*,
Bund, Cologne
Spyropoulos,G.,and Fragnière,G.,(1991) ,*Work and Social Policies in the New
European Interuniversity Press, Brussels
Revkin,A.,(1990), *The Burning Season*, Collins, London
Williams,H.,(1988), *Whale Nation*, Jonothan Cape, London